The Psychology of Information Security

Resolving conflicts between security compliance and human behaviour

GW00578062

The Psychology of Information Security

Resolving conflicts between security compliance and human behaviour

LERON ZINATULLIN

IT Governance Publishing

IT Governance Publishing
IT Governance Limited
Unit 3, Clive Court
Bartholomew's Walk
Cambridgeshire Business Park
Ely, Cambridgeshire
CB7 4EA
United Kingdom
www.itgovernance.co.uk

First published in the United Kingdom in 2016
by IT Governance Publishing

ISBN 978-1-84928-789-0

FOREWORD

So often information security is viewed as a technical discipline – a world of firewalls, antivirus software, access controls and encryption; an opaque and enigmatic discipline which defies understanding, with a priesthood who often protect their profession with complex concepts, language and, most of all, secrecy.

Leron takes a practical, pragmatic and no-holds-barred approach to demystifying the topic. He reminds us that ultimately security depends on people – and that we all act in what we see as our rational self-interest – sometimes ill-informed, ill-judged, even downright perverse.

No approach to security can ever succeed without considering people – and as a profession we need to look beyond our computers to understand the business, the culture of the organisation, and, most of all, how we can create a security environment which helps people feel free to actually do their job.

David Ferbrache OBE, FBCS

Technical Director, Cyber Security

KPMG UK

PREFACE

In his book *How to Win Friends and Influence People*, Dale Carnegie tells a story about George B. Johnston of Enid, Oklahoma. Mr Johnston was responsible for safety at an engineering company. Among other duties he had to ensure that employees were wearing their hard hats while on the job. His common strategy was to spot people who didn't follow this policy, approach them, quote the regulation and insist on compliance. He succeeded in having them abide by the rules, but only temporarily: employees usually removed their hats as soon as he left.

He decided to try something new. Instead of referring to them with a lot of authority, he tried to be genuinely interested in the workers' comfort. He wanted to know if the hats were uncomfortable enough to prevent people from wearing them.

Also, instead of simply insisting on following the policy, he mentioned to the employees that it was important to wear hard hats, because they were designed to prevent injuries and this was in their best interest. As a result, this not only increased compliance, but also mitigated resentment towards the regulation.

Information security professionals are faced with a similar problem. They have to ensure that a company is adequately addressing information security risks, but they also have to communicate the value of security appropriately in order to be successful.

On the one hand, not putting security controls in place may result in significant losses for an organisation. On the other hand, badly implemented security mechanisms may obstruct employees' productivity and result in a poor security culture.

Security professionals and users may share different views on security-related activities. In order to ensure that users in the organisation comply with policies, security professionals should also consider employees' behaviour.

The main goal of this book is to gain insight into information security issues related to human behaviour, from both end-users' and security professionals' perspectives. It aims to provide a set of recommendations to support the security professional's decision-making process when implementing controls and communicating these changes within an organisation. To achieve this, a number of interviews were conducted with UK-based security professionals from various sectors, including financial services, advertising, media, energy and technology. Their views, along with further relevant research, were incorporated into the book, in order to provide a holistic overview of the problem and propose a solution.

ABOUT THE AUTHOR

Leron Zinatullin is an experienced risk consultant, specialising in cyber security strategy, management and delivery. He has led large-scale, global, high-value security transformation projects with a view to improving cost performance and supporting business strategy.

He has extensive knowledge and practical experience in solving information security, privacy and architectural issues across multiple industry sectors.

He has an MSc in Information Security from University College London, where he focused on the human aspects of information security. His research was related to modelling conflicts between security compliance and human behaviour.

Website: *zinatullin.com*

Twitter: @le_rond

ACKNOWLEDGEMENTS

I would like to thank the many people who helped me with this book; those who provided support, talked things over, offered comments and assisted in the editing.

CONTENTS

Contents

CHAPTER 1: INTRODUCTION TO INFORMATION SECURITY

Information security encompasses many aspects of business, including financial controls, human resources and protection of the physical environment, as well as health and safety measures. But who are security professionals? What skills do they have?

I asked these questions of Javvad Malik, security advocate and blogger, during one of our lunches. I met Javvad at a security conference in London. He helped me to prepare for my first talk at said conference, sharing his views and experience on the security industry. He also expressed his vision on this subject: "When I was starting in the field, nobody really knew what security was," he said. "Then came the perception that it was all about hackers working from their mums' basements. Then, they were assumed to be IT specialists, and then that they were specialists who didn't necessarily know much about IT but who knew more regulation and legislation. And now everyone is just confused."

A security professional is responsible for protecting a company against cyber threats. However, security itself is very broad. It is similar to medicine: there are general practitioners who know a little bit about everything, which is the base level of knowledge. For complex cases they will refer you to specialists in blood, heart, eyes, ears and other specific body parts. The same applies to security. There are broad generalists and technical experts. There are also non-technical security professionals, who understand the business, the risks and how to integrate security into the corporate strategy. Additionally, there are product- or technology-specific experts who can help to tune events and incident management systems, or forensically investigate platforms. Just as you can't replace a surgeon with a GP, you can't replace a technical subject-matter expert with a generalist, and vice versa.

Information security issues in organisations were being raised long before the rapid development of technology. Companies have always been concerned with protecting their confidential information, including their intellectual property and trade secrets. In other words, all organisations have *assets*, which help a company to generate revenue. Hence the goal of information security is to identify and protect these assets.

The world of information security rests on three pillars: confidentiality, availability and integrity.

Confidentiality is crucial to any company, because it ensures that a secret remains a secret so that intellectual property, such as trading algorithms, engineering designs or client records, is protected against competitors.

Security professionals also have to find a balance between securing sensitive information and also making it *available* to the people who need it. There is no point in having data that can't be accessed. Denial-of-service attacks can be a popular tactic employed by attackers to impede the business. This becomes especially important if it is conducted online, as in the case of e-commerce websites.

Integrity ensures that information remains unaltered during transmission or storage unless required. Attackers may want to interfere with bank transactions, for example, because modifying a single digit in an account number can compromise everything.

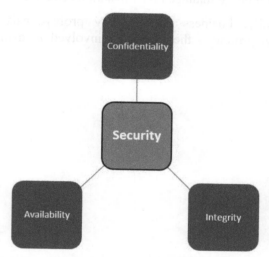

Figure 1: Three pillars of information security

These three pillars must be linked back to business requirements. In order to do that, information security professionals should identify the relevant assets, for which confidentiality, availability and integrity are a critical requirement. Engaging business stakeholders can help to identify these assets. In other words, the business defines what needs to be protected. It is up to security professionals to determine which appropriate measures are required and to communicate them in business terms.

It is here that security professionals face their first challenge: the language of the business and the language of information security are different, and it is their responsibility to manage this translation effectively.

Thankfully, business and security professionals have common ground – they are both involved in managing risk.

CHAPTER 2: RISK MANAGEMENT

From the information security perspective, the people, processes and technology supporting the business are not bulletproof, and their *vulnerabilities* may be exploited. This scenario is called a *threat,* which has a certain *impact* on a company's assets.

$$\text{Impact} = \text{Vulnerability} \times \text{Threat}$$

Threats vary in probability and therefore the degree of impact. For example, in a company which handles customers' personal data online, the probability of human error leading to disclosure of sensitive information might be greater and have a larger business impact than someone bringing down the website.

Additionally, the exploitation of a vulnerable critical system may have a greater impact than that of one used purely for archiving.

This relationship defines *risk*.

$$\text{Risk} = \text{Probability} \times \text{Impact}$$

In order to reduce the probability and impact of the threat, information security professionals can implement countermeasures, otherwise known as controls.

When thinking in terms of protection measures, it is useful to know who the attackers are. Security professionals should understand that attackers are people too, who differ in resources, motivation, ability and risk propensity. According to Bruce Schneier, author of *Beyond Fear*,[1] the categories of attacker are:

- **Opportunists**: The most common type of attacker. As the category indicates, they spot and seize an 'opportunity' and are convinced that they will not get caught. It is easy to deter such attackers via cursory countermeasures.

- **Emotional attackers**: They may accept a high level of risk and usually want to make a statement through their attack. The most common motivation for them is revenge against an organisation due to actual or perceived injustice. Although emotional attackers feel powerful when causing harm, they sometimes 'hope to get caught' as a way of solving the issues they were unhappy with but were unable to change from the beginning.

- **Cold intellectual attackers**: Skilled and resourceful professionals who attack for their own gain or are employed to do so. They target information, not the system, and often use insiders to get it. Unlike opportunists, cold intellectual attackers are not discouraged by cursory countermeasures.

- **Terrorists**: They accept high risk to gain visibility and make a statement. Not only are they hard to deter

---

[1] Bruce Schneier, *Beyond Fear: Thinking Sensibly about Security in an Uncertain World*, Copernicus Books, 2003.

by cursory countermeasures, but they can even see them as a thrill.

- **Friends and relations**: They may introduce a problem to both individuals (in the form of financial fraud, for example) and companies (by abusing authorisation credentials provided to legitimate employees). In this scenario, a victim and an attacker are sharing physical space, which makes it very easy to gain login and other sensitive information.

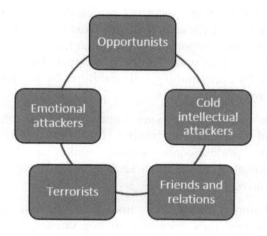

Figure 2: Categories of attackers

Information security vulnerabilities, threats and risks are part of today's corporate world, and are just as relevant and important to information security specialists as to the business.

2: Risk Management

Information security professionals are comfortable thinking in terms of threats and vulnerabilities, but the focus of risk management should be on assets, not threats. Focusing solely on security regardless of the business's needs can be counterproductive.

Information security should support and enable the business – as such, security professionals must consider the cost aspect of implementing countermeasures. They should implement the controls ensuring that the cost is appropriate for the asset to which it is applied.

Many information security professionals view risk negatively and believe that all risk must be removed. It is, however, also important to communicate the positive aspects of risk as well. Threats in this paradigm could be replaced by opportunities, vulnerabilities by strengths and impact by benefits.

Despite this negative view, operational risk-taking is required in order to realise business opportunities. Security professionals should make a habit of communicating information security risks to the business in a positive way.

For example, employees may believe that security professionals' only priority is to stop viruses, in order to prevent widespread infection across the network. In reality, there is also a valid business reason for such activities. Security team members therefore have to go a step further and demonstrate that virus prevention can also increase the availability of resources and the productivity of employees, because they can focus on their work rather than waiting for their laptop to be cleared of malicious software (malware).

2: Risk Management

Among other concerns, business personnel may care about enabling business opportunities or enhancing brand reputation and trust. In order to find out what their priorities are, security professionals must engage them to collect business drivers, goals and objectives and understand how they can support the business.

A clear link should be preserved between business concerns and countermeasures so that security professionals can demonstrate the value they bring.

Business teams are much more likely to accept this perspective, because doing business means taking risks and exploiting opportunities. Therefore a company's *risk appetite* must be determined.

To determine the risk appetite, one should understand that security risk is just one of the many types of risk that a business faces on a day-to-day basis: socio-economic, financial, geopolitical, legal and personnel are just a few examples. Any of these may be a higher priority to the company than security, which security professionals should bear in mind. Based on this prioritisation, a company can define an acceptable level of risk under which to operate.

It is perfectly normal to accept the risk that falls below this threshold.

Treating information security risks as another facet of the business can yield great results. For example, SWOT and PEST analyses can be performed to broaden the view of risk.

SWOT stands for Strengths, Weaknesses, Opportunities and Threats. It is a simple technique, which involves listing external and internal factors that are helpful and harmful for an organisation.

	Helpful	Harmful
Internal	Strengths	Weaknesses
External	Opportunities	Threats

Figure 3: SWOT analysis

When performing this analysis in a security context, one should consider using the strengths both to exploit opportunities and to confront threats.

For example, a business partner would be reassured in the safety of doing business with a company if said company had implemented adequate security measures, which also mitigate the risk of cyber attacks. Effective security can therefore lead to the additional benefit of increasing trust and, as a result, sales.

One should also consider mitigating weaknesses that might be exploited by threats. For instance, adopting a vulnerability management programme ensures that the latest updates are applied to a company's software, by addressing known flaws.

Similarly, security professionals should also search for ways of strengthening weaknesses that might hinder the exploration of opportunities.

For example, an e-commence provider which has developed their own internal cloud solution may wish to grow their business by marketing such a product to external customers. However, vulnerabilities present in the solution might negatively impact their reputation if compromised. Therefore, investing in patching these flaws would enable the business to expand.

In order to focus on the broader external factors, security professionals can also utilise the PEST analysis. It takes Political, Economic, Social and Technological factors into consideration. Here is an example:

Political	Economic	Social	Technological
Trade restrictions Political stability in foreign partner countries New environmental law	Inflation rate Exchange rate Economic downturn	Culture Population growth Age distribution Change	Innovation Process automation

Figure 4: PEST analysis

There are variations of this tool which include other factors, such as legal or environmental. Performing this analysis enables security professionals to see the bigger picture of enterprise-wide risks. This, in turn, encourages early identification of potential risk treatment options, like countermeasures, in a proactive manner.

These tools and techniques are a good start, but in order to appreciate an example of applied risk management, I interviewed Thom Langford, Chief Information Security

2: Risk Management

Officer at Publicis Groupe, and asked his opinion on this subject. Thom has delivered a number of industry presentations on information security and his pragmatic view on this subject will summarise this discussion on risk management and provide some real-life case studies.

"I think everybody has a view on risk management, and it is not always a good one", he started, "Traditionally, risks are seen as bad and have to be removed. They never change and the same risks are going to be there all the time."

He described a conventional approach where everything is perceived as static and security professionals live in the world of spreadsheets: "You list your risks in them, you list what you are going to do about them, how you are going to measure them, and then you decide whether you've fixed them or not."

That attitude has changed drastically for him in the last four years: "If you act this way, the business will be stifled quite dramatically because of your security implementations." Any measure that completely disregards the nature of the business and its context will become an obstacle, or even be counterproductive.

"All you are doing is reducing the ability of the business to work effectively because you don't see the big picture of how it operates."

If security professionals can connect the benefits of a security program to the ability of a company to increase sales, to safely enter riskier markets, to give assurance to their clients and to bring confidence to the industry, then they are truly adding value to the business. If security professionals are just doing security for security's sake, they go back to stifling the business rather than supporting it.

"If you haven't even read your company's annual report," – Langford continues, "how do you know what your security programme is supporting?"

"If you haven't attended a shareholder meeting or an earnings call, you can't really know what you are doing. If you don't understand what the core purpose of the business is, how can you actually align your security with it?"

Security professionals should talk to as many people as possible across the business. For instance, if they are ensuring successful security implementation at a manufacturing plant, they could start by talking to the people on the factory floor to see how they operate.

The aim for security professionals is to understand what others do and how they do it, as well as what others need from security and their level of security awareness.

If, for example, the shift manager tells a security professional that smokers are leaving the doors open to have their cigarette break then he is understandably concerned about the risk of theft. As another example, a manager notices that her computer is running slow and strange pop-up messages are appearing. At first glance, these appear to be small issues, but potentially important ones which a security professional could assist with.

Security professionals should also try to understand what the business needs from security. As an example, a CFO's primary goal may be to ensure that she's able to get reports and the payroll out on a monthly basis. She might find herself staying awake at night worrying that the systems will go down, which would allow security professionals to focus on the integrity and availability of the data, prioritising disaster recovery and business continuity.

Solving such problems, perceived or otherwise, can start to build advocates for security. If the people aspect of security is not considered, there is a good chance that the security solution, no matter how perfect it is, may be blocked by the business.

CHAPTER 3: THE COMPLEXITY OF RISK MANAGEMENT

We talked about risk management in the previous chapter, but it is important to understand it in the context of human behaviour. Security professionals should recognise that people perceive risk differently, and that this affects their behaviour.

For example, Daniel Kahneman and Amos Tversky in their research present several choice problems, demonstrating the complexity of situations where people are faced with uncertainty.[2]

In one of the scenarios the researchers gave the participants 1,000 Israeli pounds and asked if they would prefer to give 500 pounds back and keep the remaining 500 for themselves. The second option was to flip a coin where they would win the full amount for heads or lose the full amount for tails.

The majority of the participants chose the safe option of receiving a guaranteed 500 pounds.

In the second scenario, the participants were given 2,000 pounds and were presented with a similar choice. This time, they could choose to either give 500 pounds back, or to flip a coin where they could lose 1,000 or win the entire pot.

---

[2] Daniel Kahneman and Amos Tversky, "Prospect Theory: An Analysis of Decision under Risk", *Econometrica*, 47(2), March 1979, 263–291.

The majority of the participants chose the second option.

This demonstrates that there are different psychological associations with gains and losses: people have a tendency to be risk-averse to protect perceived gains and at the same time they are willing to take extra risk to recover perceived losses.

This makes it more difficult for a security professional to communicate the value of security to business stakeholders, as they tend to downplay the importance of security risks.

Insurance companies, for example, face a similar issue: businesses think that paying for insurance now is throwing money away, as it's a gamble as to whether they will need to cash in. Whereas spending nothing on the cover is a guaranteed saving.

Ironically enough, spending money now to mitigate or transfer the risk is a logical risk assessment and the true gamble is to do nothing and wait for an incident to occur.

Asymmetric perception of gains and losses is not the only reason for the additional complexity of decision-making – the perception of risk can also be clouded by people's past experiences and expectations.

John Adams's research suggests that "the risk manager must … deal not only with risk perceived through science, but also with virtual risk – risks where the science is inconclusive and people are thus liberated to argue from, and act upon, pre-established beliefs, convictions, prejudices and superstitions".[3]

To illustrate an individual's decision-making process while dealing with risk, Adams introduces a concept called a *risk thermostat*. The premise is that people vary in their propensity to take risks, which is influenced by their perception, the potential reward and prior experience of loss.

Indeed, if someone experienced a negative event in the past, they assign a disproportionately high probability and impact to that situation compared to an unknown event, even if probability theory tells us otherwise.

On the other hand, people tend to overestimate spectacular but rare risks, but downplay common risks, which can be as harmful for the company, if not more so.

Gary Klein, in his book *Streetlights and Shadows: Searching for the Keys to Adaptive Decision Making*,[4] suggests that risk management plans do not guarantee success and may result in a false sense of safety, actually increasing risk. Adams supports this point referring to the phenomenon of risk compensation, where introducing safety measures makes people engage in more risky behaviour.

---

[3] John Adams, "Risk Management: It's Not Rocket Science … It's Much More Complicated", *Risk Management*, 54(5), 2007, 36–40.

[4] Gary Klein, *Streetlights and Shadows: Searching for the Keys to Adaptive Decision Making*, MIT Press, 2009.

For example, seat belts can save a life in a crash, so people buckle up and take more risks when driving, leading to an increased number of accidents. As a result, the overall number of deaths remains unchanged.

Security professionals can observe similar convictions in their companies: "we have a firewall, so we must be secure".

The complexities of human behaviour as it relates to risk management are compounded by additional complexities of risk identification. This is illustrated by Nasim Taleb in his book *The Black Swan*,[5] where the concept that some events cannot be predicted, even with unlimited resources, is introduced.

One example of such an event can be found in the title of the book itself. Prior to the discovery of the Australian continent, scientists believed that, after years of observation, all swans were white. In their limited realm of experience, they did not consider that there could be any other type of swan living in the world. Therefore, when explorers encountered the black swan species variation in Australia it was an unexpected, unpredictable event. This demonstrates that empirical evidence is not sufficient to confidently predict the absence of outliers.

To demonstrate that such events can have a great impact, Taleb provides examples of Mirage Casino's four largest losses. These included an unsuccessful attempt to bomb the casino, a ransom demand for the owner's kidnapped

---

[5] Nassim Nicholas Taleb, *The Black Swan: The Impact of the Highly Improbable Fragility*, Vol. 2. Random House, 2010.

daughter, a fine due to negligence in completing tax returns and a tiger mauling.

How many of these risks could have been foreseen and managed appropriately, preventing such losses in the first place?

Instead of properly assessing those risks with low probability and high impact, casinos tend to focus their efforts on high-probability, low-impact events, such as preventing cheating at the tables.

Thorough risk assessment and identification is not the only challenge; there may also be unforeseen consequences of taking action to address risks that can have devastating effects.

As an example, the manager of a nightclub may be concerned by recent diminishing revenue. He regularly observes many people inside the club, but the profits from the entrance fees are lower than expected.

The manager initially suspects that employee fraud is to blame; however, after investigating further, it turns out that only a few customers were entering via the front door and paying for their ticket. As soon as they get in, they let their friends in through the fire escape.

He therefore may choose to prevent this behaviour by jamming the fire exit doors shut, without considering the increased risk to health and safety for his employees and guests as a direct result of his actions.

This, of course, can lead to a tragedy and subsequent loss of life in the event of a fire.

3: The Complexity of Risk Management

The Sherwood Applied Business Security Architecture (SABSA) Institute provides a less dramatic example of risk interaction. According to their framework,[6] accountability for risk should be delegated to individuals who are subject-matter experts.

A CFO, for instance, might be interested in maximising profits by gambling on the markets, regardless of compliance. A head of compliance, on the other hand, is concerned with potential fines for violating regulations. They can escalate the risk to the CEO, whose responsibility it is to make a decision on which course of action to take.

Such an approach demonstrates that identification of risks is not enough: each risk should have a person who is accountable for it. If the business believes that security professionals are responsible for closing the doors, they will leave them open.

Everything that has been discussed so far makes the job of a security professional much more challenging. After all, Adams states that "risk management is not rocket science – it's much more complicated."

This doesn't mean, however, that risk management should be abandoned. Quite the contrary; a wider group of stakeholders should be engaged. Information security professionals should understand how information security risks interact with other business risks.

---

[6] John Sherwood, Andrew Clark and David Lynas, "Enterprise Security Architecture White Paper", 2009.

3: The Complexity of Risk Management

Managing stakeholders and communication is therefore becoming one of the most essential skills for a security professional.

CHAPTER 4: STAKEHOLDERS AND COMMUNICATION

As discussed in the previous chapter, stakeholder engagement is key in making sure that risks are addressed properly. The earlier people are involved in a security project, the easier it is to obtain their support. The same principle applies when security professionals have to be involved in other people's projects. Andrew Martin, a director for IT risk at a global bank, shares an example of a security solution that was not successfully implemented. A company wanted to mitigate the risk of exploiting vulnerabilities in their applications and decided to deploy a code-scanning tool. This would make sure that applications are tested for exploits before they are released.

"Uptake on the use of this code-scanning tool was low due to challenges with communication with the development teams that would need to use the tool," he says; "the impacted teams weren't sufficiently trained on the use of the tool and there wasn't enough support from management of the development teams to use it."

Development teams have very tight timelines and budgets to work to in order to meet the business objectives. Anything that could disrupt these aspects is viewed with caution.

As a result, applications that should have had their code scanned either hadn't, or had to be scanned at a much later stage of the development cycle. In either case, the risk of having applications with flaws in them was elevated.

Given that some applications weren't scanned, or had significant delays in the scanning, some bugs could exist which were not addressed.

These new or enhanced applications were being delivered to facilitate revenue growth or streamline exiting processes to reduce cost and complexity.

The impact on the business was that the new functionality they were expecting took longer to materialise, resulting in users' frustration.

Communicating new security policies, tools and practices to impacted teams is absolutely critical. This is especially important in large organisations with many technology stakeholder groups spread across multiple geographies.

Martin provides the following recommendations to prevent such situations from happening:

1. Articulate the benefits. Security and risk teams need to ensure they position any new processes or tools in a way that highlights the benefits to each stakeholder group.
2. Provide clear steps. In order to ensure the change is successful, security professionals should clearly outline the steps for how to start realising these benefits.
3. Communicate frequently and at the right level. Communication must start at the top of an organisation and work its way down, so that priorities and expectations can be aligned. A person may need to hear the same message multiple times before they take action.

4: Stakeholders and Communication

Information security professionals first have to understand who the stakeholders are and how to keep them engaged.

In his research, Freeman suggests that "a stakeholder in an organization is (by definition) any group or individual who can affect or is affected by the achievement of the organization's objectives".[7]

Mitchell and his colleagues build on these and other findings. They recommend a theory of stakeholder identification in their study,[8] which is based on three variables: power, legitimacy and urgency.

They refer to *urgency* as "the degree to which stakeholder claims call for immediate attention". It is determined not only by time constraints, but also by the significance of the relationship.

Power in this context is defined as the ability to influence decision-making in a company by material or social means.[9]

Legitimacy refers to those stakeholders who have a formal structure in place with which to affect the project or organisation. Examples of such stakeholders may include

---

[7] R. Edward Freeman and John McVea, "A Stakeholder Approach to Strategic Management", 2001.

[8] Ronald K. Mitchell, Bradley R. Agle and Donna J. Wood, "Toward a Theory of Stakeholder Identification and Salience: Defining the Principle of Who and What Really Counts", *Academy of Management Review*, 22(4), 1997, 853–886.

[9] Amitai Etzioni, *Moral Dimension: Toward a New Economics*, Simon and Schuster, 2010.

heads of departments, or those who sit on the Board of Directors.

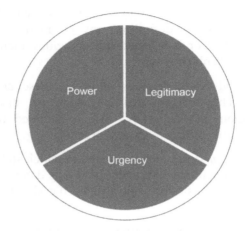

Figure 5: Stakeholder salience

Security professionals should prepare a communications plan to ensure that nobody is left out and stakeholders' interests are considered.

As a first step when creating the plan, a stakeholder register should be created which captures their contact information. It should also include the feedback received during the types of discussion with your stakeholders to try to understand their business needs that were suggested by Langford in Chapter 2. Table 1 can help with documenting the expectations of the project, requirements and other comments.

4: Stakeholders and Communication

Table 1: Stakeholder register

Name	Job title	Contact Information	Expectation	Requirements	Influence	Comments

The influence column should contain relevant information regarding the power, legitimacy and urgency of the corresponding stakeholder.

As soon as the stakeholders are identified and recorded, security professionals should engage them in order to understand their preferred method of communication, its desired frequency, and the responsibility and the level of detail that they expect. They should then assign responsibilities for involving each stakeholder to a specific member of the project team.

Table 2: Communications plan

What to communicate	Why	Preferred method	Responsibility	Frequency

There are, however, complexities with keeping this sort of information. For example, stakeholders may want to prevent this table being disclosed to people with competing stakes. Therefore the security professional should apply extra care in handling this data.

Stakeholder engagement and communication planning can make security-related projects run much more smoothly, because security professionals spend almost all of their time communicating in various ways.

Communication can be viewed as a simple model, consisting of three parts: a sender, a receiver and a channel.

Figure 6: Simple communication model

Regardless of the simplicity of this model, many errors can occur. The cause of these errors lies in the way that we process and interpret information.

The sender 'encodes' the original message and relays it to the receiver. The resulting message may be different from what was intended, not only due to its dependency on the sender's communication skills, but also because the receiver interprets the message based on her own values and past experiences.

A Chinese whispers game played by children all over the world serves as a good illustration of this principle.

4: Stakeholders and Communication

Our perception of information is based on the filters that we develop during childhood, which are formed as a result of our cultural and social background. Moreover, our brain, in an effort to process information in a more efficient manner, constantly omits and generalises our experiences, which can lead to miscommunication.

Security professionals have to be aware of their assumptions. Understanding past experiences and how they affect the communication and decision-making process helps to build important self-awareness. This is the first step in developing effective communication skills, such as active listening.

Active listening is one of the most important, yet underappreciated, communication techniques. Despite common belief, it doesn't only involve reiterating messages and asking semi-relevant questions. It actually happens on a deeper level.

When listening actively, one tries to understand the real problem by not jumping to conclusions and eagerly attempting to propose a solution too soon. Listening in this manner expends a great deal of mental effort, and prevents tunnel vision around our own assumptions and stereotypes.

One must be fully engaged in the present conversation, which requires minimising all external distractions, such as phone and emails, as well as making sure that the message is understood. Additionally, particular word choices, tone of voice, gestures and facial expressions can be useful non-verbal cues.

In fact, research suggests that tone of voice, gestures and other non-verbal factors carry much more meaning for humans than actual words.[10] This could be due to the evolution of our fight-or-flight decision-making processes, which have developed over millennia by reading body language.

Active listening incorporates both verbal and non-verbal aspects of communication. This can help security professionals to understand business users, which in turn would be valuable both in implementing security policies and in gaining the necessary support.

To explore this question further, I interviewed Jitender Arora, Information Security and Risk Executive at a major bank. His experience in managing large-scale global information security programmes as a chief information security officer will help us to better understand the issues related to stakeholder management.

"One thing I always do in any programme," he begins, "is approach stakeholders, including user groups, in their working environment, and make them feel comfortable."

He builds rapport as a first step, then suggests using active listening to gain insight into your stakeholders' problems, their preferences, what they would like to retain and what they would wish to modify. By approaching any change from a psychological perspective and encouraging stakeholder involvement, people feel that they have largely contributed to the creation and design of the

---

[10] Albert Mehrabian and Susan R. Ferris, "Inference of Attitudes from Nonverbal Communication in Two Channels", *Journal of Consulting Psychology*, 31(3), 1967, 248–252.

security changes. As a result, security professionals will gain advocates in support of the programme and prevent blockers, which are critical success factors for any such engagement.

At the end of the day, security professionals help to make the business secure. This can be achieved more easily when people cooperate with the security team, rather than trying to sabotage the project.

Arora also supports this point. He argues that security mechanisms usually change the way that people operate.

"A very simple example would be when implementing a control in terms of how people access production systems. If you go into an organisation in which their practices have been acceptable for the past ten years, and you suddenly tell them that they can no longer follow the same practice, you are, in a way, taking a privilege away from them and they will react accordingly."

Arora uses the following analogy: "If I suddenly tell my son, who normally watches one hour of TV a day for the past several years, that he cannot watch it without asking permission every time, and not more than thirty minutes from now on, he will not like it and will most likely rebel and show his displeasure."

In order to avoid such reactionary behaviour, a change in control implementation must be managed appropriately and mapped to policies, which have been aligned to the business drivers and supported by senior management. We will cover this in more detail in the next chapter.

CHAPTER 5: INFORMATION SECURITY GOVERNANCE

In today's corporations, information security professionals have a lot on their plate. While facing constantly evolving cyber threats, they must comply with numerous laws and regulations, protect the company's assets and mitigate risks to the furthest extent possible. In order to successfully address these concerns, they must first establish desired practices which form the basis of company policies.

In a traditional sense, a *policy* is a document that provides a high-level overview of how company processes should operate in a secure manner. It defines the goal of the information security programme, which in turn supports the business strategy and vision. It also serves a number of other purposes such as defining roles and responsibilities and demonstrating the commitment of senior management.

Such a high-level approach can be very beneficial in cases where a security professional wishes to describe the value of security to a board of directors, but it may also have some serious limitations. The information contained can be too vague, or not well enough understood, to allow a particular control to be easily implemented. For example, stating that the network must be protected does not provide the necessary detail for a network security administrator to configure a firewall. It is common to find that many security policies are not followed simply because they are not fully understood.

Standards can be used to regulate the approach to security across an organisation, preventing a company from implementing conflicting or redundant solutions across various branches or departments.

A security professional might consider creating a set of *guidelines* to support the standards. Guidelines are not mandatory; they simply outline a set of best practices, which people are encouraged to follow.

Security professionals will usually have to create a series of *procedures*, i.e. a set of basic steps which aids the implementation of policies and standards.

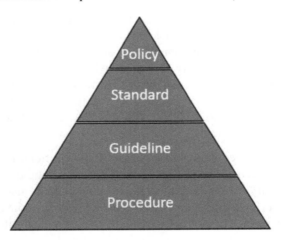

Figure 7: Policy hierarchy

For the purpose of this book, we will refer to all these documents as security policies.

5: Information Security Governance

A good starting point for developing a security policy is the ISO 27001 standard. The ISO 27001 standard is a document that provides guidance on managing the risk associated with threats to confidentiality, integrity and the availability of organisation's assets. These assets, as defined in ISO 27001, include people, software, hardware and services. According to the standard, secure operation of the business can be achieved through the creation and maintenance of an information security management system, which is a framework for risk management. It is usually supported by a set of information security policies.

Well-established frameworks such as ISO 27001 can be useful for implementing good practices and controls. However, using them purely as they appear on paper without adapting them to the company's specific characteristics can have negative consequences.

Security professionals might only stick to the standard simply to achieve certification and demonstrate compliance. But, as Langford, who shared his vision on risk management in Chapter 2, puts it, "compliance doesn't equal security". A company may be unaware of risky practices its employees engage in, or may be implementing unnecessary controls dictated by the standard that might hinder the business's performance. It may also contrast with the CEO's perspective, whose goal focuses on driving the business and not necessarily on achieving 100% compliance.

A study by Anttila and Kajava supports this point.[11] It focuses on determining how beneficial to a business the implementation of security frameworks is, such as ISO 27001. The main problem is that such standards are too high-level and have an "abstract control definition", which "leaves space for interpretation". Furthermore, the study illustrates that many companies focus solely on obtaining formal certification rather than implementing security controls that cater to their business needs. This research therefore reveals the difficulties of measuring business benefits, which result from the implementation of security standards such as ISO 27001.

Another study by Sharma and Dash concludes that ISO 27001 does not provide detailed guidance and requires substantial levels of expertise to implement.[12] Moreover, the authors claim, "If risk assessment is flawed, implementers don't have sufficient security and risk assessment expertise or do not have the management and organisational commitment to implement security, then it is perfectly possible to be fully compliant with the standard, but be insecure."

Their research supports the previous assertion that organisations have a tendency to implement information

[11] Juhani Anttila and Jorma Kajava, "Challenging IS and ISM Standardization for Business Benefits", delivered at ARES '10 International Conference on Availability, Reliability, and Security, 2010.

[12] Dr N K Sharma and Prabir Kumar Dash, "Effectiveness of ISO 27001, as an Information Security Management System: An Analytical Study of Financial Aspects", *Far East Journal of Psychology and Business*, 9(5), 2012, 57–71.

security controls mainly to comply with legal and regulatory requirements. The consequence is that such implementations demonstrate poor return on investment.

Langford also has an opinion on the ISO 27001 standard: "I think compliance is extremely useful, but it is not the be-all and end-all," he says. "If all you are trying to do is to get the certification, you're only engaging in security theatre.[13] You're only doing what is required to get the auditor happy and you are ticking things off and writing procedures, but nobody really knows anything about it. Nobody is paying any actual attention to it, apart from that one day in which you make sure that the right people are in the right office, and the auditor has that long lunch that you need. So it's a start, but it is not the way to go.

"An example of that is a risk register that is only looked at once a year: that is compliance. A risk register should be looked at on a regular basis to ascertain that risks haven't changed, or if likelihoods haven't changed, or that the exploitations have changed, if risk appetites have changed within the organisation, for example. If it becomes a living and breathing document, then you are looking more at a risk-based approach to security. If it's just a mechanical once-a-year, tick-tick-tick format, then you are in a compliance environment."

When creating a security policy, security professionals might choose a standard framework to work from, but

---

[13] "Security theater is the practice of investing in countermeasures intended to provide the feeling of improved security while doing little or nothing to actually achieve it". Schneier, *Beyond Fear*, 38.

they should do so only as a starting point. How can specialists adapt the policy of a specific company while keeping the business's interests at heart?

Arora, who shared his opinion in the previous chapter, proves to be useful in the context of governance as well.

He suggests that the accessibility of security policies is one of the key factors that determine success in a business setting: "The first thing I do in any organisation," Arora says, "is that I visit their homepage and type in 'information security'. If the policy doesn't come up as the first search result, something is wrong. If people can't find the security policy, how can you expect them to read it? How can you expect them to comply?"

According to him, a security professional can conduct a simple survey, by posing three questions to the business community:

- Do you know that we have an information security department?
- Do you know the services this department has to offer?
- Do you know how to contact them if you need it?

The results might be eye-opening.

This shouldn't come as a surprise – corporate policies are consistently mentioned as being the greatest cause of dissatisfaction in the workplace.

5: Information Security Governance

Frederick Herzberg and colleagues, in the book *The Motivation to Work*,[14] list 'hygiene' factors that are related to employees' job satisfaction. His research suggests that a corporate policy tends to demotivate people.

It is an interesting lab finding, but does it hold true in a real company? Sadly, it does.

Herzberg's findings were tested at Texas Instruments Incorporated. M. Scott Myers describes a survey conducted by the management of the company.[15]

A random selection of 282 scientists, engineers, manufacturing supervisors, technicians and assemblers were chosen from within the Dallas divisions. Each staff member was asked to think of a time when they felt exceptionally good or exceptionally bad about their job, either in the past or the present. The participants would describe a favourable and unfavourable circumstance and whether the effect on their emotions was long-lasting.

The results demonstrate that achievement was the most popular category, counting for a third of all responses. Interestingly, *company policy and administration*, which can be thought of as the perception of an organisation's goals, procedures and practices, was expressed in an unfavourable manner four times more frequently than in a favourable one.

---

[14] Frederick Herzberg, Bernard Mausner and Barbara Bloch Snyderman, *The Motivation to Work*, new edn: Transaction, 1993.
[15] M. Scott Myers, "Who Are Your Motivated Workers?", *Harvard Business Review*, 1964, 73–88.

With this in mind, let's discuss the specific challenges of a security policy implementation based on the ISO 27001 standard.

CHAPTER 6: PROBLEMS WITH POLICIES

In their book *Competing for the Future*,[16] Hamel and Prahalad describe an experiment in which a group of researchers observed monkeys' behaviour. Five monkeys were put in a room with bananas hanging from the ceiling. A pole was placed in the middle to access the bananas.

Each time a monkey tried to climb the pole, the rest of the monkeys were soaked with cold water. After a few repetitions, the monkeys started to physically reprimand whoever climbed the pole. Naturally, no monkey dared to go up the pole again.

Scientists then took one of the monkeys out of the room and replaced it with another one. The new monkey saw the bananas and tried to reach them by climbing the pole, but was disciplined immediately by the others. Although confused, the new member learned not to climb the pole.

A second monkey was then substituted with a new one and the story repeated. Eventually, all of the monkeys were replaced by new ones. Although none of these monkeys had themselves received a cold shower, they continued to deter anyone who attempted to reach the bananas. Without having received a cold shower themselves, the monkeys accepted the fact that things are done in a particular way.

---

[16] Gary Hamel and Coimbatore K. Prahalad, *Competing for the Future*, Harvard Business Press, 2013.

Security professionals might develop similar behaviour if they don't challenge the existing status quo and don't ask why policies are implemented in the first place.

As we discussed in the previous chapter, when policies are put in place without any clear guidance or further scrutiny, a business can develop problems. Although it may seem to comply with all relevant regulations, beneath the surface users might be struggling to perform their core business activities and may be forced to violate those poorly implemented security policies.

Let's consider a situation where the security professional is required to develop a policy that will protect an investment bank from malicious code.

According to the "Controls against malicious code" section of ISO 27001, "detection, prevention and recovery controls to protect against malicious code and appropriate user awareness procedures should be implemented".

The following section provides a list of policies recommended by the standard. It also presents scenarios that demonstrate how these controls impact employees' behaviour.

1. A policy that outlines a list of authorised software that can be installed on users' workstations.

In practice it might mean that if users wish to install a piece of software which is not on the authorised list, they must gain formal written approval from the security manager.

Here's how this policy affected John, an analyst in the bank:

6: Problems with Policies

John is writing a report for the client. The deadline is fast approaching but he still has a lot of work ahead of him. The night before the deadline, John realises that in order to finish his work, he requires the use of a special piece of data analysis software which is not included in the list of authorised programs. He is also unable to install it on his workstation, because he doesn't have the required privileges. Getting the formal written approval from the security manager is not feasible, because it is going to take too long. John decides to copy the sensitive information required for the analysis onto his personal computer, using a flash drive, to finish the work at home, where he can install any software he wants. He understands the risk but he also wants to get the job done in order to avoid missing the deadline and get a good performance review. Unfortunately, he leaves his bag with the flash drive in the taxi on the way back home. He never tells anyone about this incident to avoid embarrassment or a reprimand.

2. A policy that restricts the use of file sharing websites and limited access to CD/DVD and USB flash drives, preventing users from obtaining files from external networks or other media.

Here is a potential implementation of this policy: if users want to obtain a specific file from the Internet or from an external device, they have to submit a written request to their manager, who will decide if this file is essential to performing their duties.

Here's how this policy affected Mary:

6: Problems with Policies

Mary is a consultant working closely with a client, an international energy company, to finalise a report on a risk analysis which she performed.

She works directly with the CFO of this company, who is very impatient and busy with other tasks.

Mary doesn't want to annoy him, because he may complain directly to her line manager. This is a very important client, which brings a large amount of revenue to the company.

The client is not aware of the new policy, which was recently implemented by the security manager, and uploads important pieces of information to a file sharing website in an encrypted archive because it is too big to transfer over corporate email.

He communicates the password to Mary over the phone and sends her the link.

Mary feels that she cannot explain the new policy to the client, but is unable to access the required files to finalise her report.

She decides to go to an Internet café during her lunch break and downloads the important file from there. She understands the risk, but believes that getting all the necessary approvals may take too long.

At the Internet café she not only downloads the encrypted files but also opens them on the café's machine to check their integrity as she does not want to have to return later in the day.

6: Problems with Policies

Because the Internet café is far from the office and she hasn't had her lunch yet, she hurries and forgets to delete the decrypted file from the machine in the Internet café.

She realises her mistake when she's back in the office, but reasons that it is not a big deal and nothing bad can happen.

3. A monthly check of users' workstations for unauthorised data and software.

If unauthorised data or software is found during such checks, the employee in question is given a warning. Repeated warnings for non-compliance with this policy can be considered potential grounds for dismissal.

Here's how this policy affected Juliet:

Juliet uses data and files obtained from various sources in her analysis. She is not sure if it is all approved or not. She's afraid to clarify this situation with the security manager due to the potential disciplinary action.

In order to avoid being caught using these files, she decides to store the information on her personal laptop.

After some time, however, she realises that it takes too long to copy and delete data from her corporate PC to her personal laptop and vice versa, and decides to process all the information, including the sensitive information, on her personal laptop.

She later takes her laptop with her on holiday, which is stolen from a public place.

4. Installation of antivirus software on each workstation, configured to perform automatic full machine scans on a daily basis to ensure that no malicious code is present.

Here is how this policy affects Robin:

Robin is a derivatives trader. Time and efficiency are critical success factors for him.

Robin carries out thousands of deals per day using his computer.

The antivirus software slows down his workstation's performance, particularly during full machine scans. This directly affects his job, as he is unable to act as fast as before and misses many valuable opportunities.

Robin understands the risk of malicious software (malware) but he is also frustrated by his inability to work as efficiently as before.

He finds a way to manually disable the antivirus on his computer.

While using the Internet, he accidentally accesses a malicious website and unwittingly introduces malware into the network.

With no antivirus software to prevent malware from stealing sensitive information from his computer, the risk of information loss is heightened.

5. Implementation of regular workshops to raise awareness of information security and train users on how to record, prevent and recover from malicious code attacks.

The programme is the same for everyone, regardless of roles and responsibilities. Employees of the organisation are showing up to the workshops and not paying attention. They cannot see the benefit of the workshops to their daily business roles. As a result, these employees are at risk of introducing malware by clicking on malicious links received via email, which could easily have been prevented.

The above examples illustrate the negative outcomes of implementing controls short-sightedly with the sole purpose of complying with the ISO 27001 standard.

When security professionals fail to scrutinise blanket controls before putting them into practice, employees may come under additional strain due to their increased workload, preventing them from performing their core business tasks, and therefore they may find ways to circumvent security measures.

Lack of clear guidance for security professionals when implementing security controls, and the fact that they have to resort to their own judgement, makes the problem even more difficult to solve.

In the above cases, the policy had an inadvertent impact on people trying to do a good job. This resulted in them putting their organisations at risk

Security professionals should start by analysing the task, and its workload implications, considering such solutions as making the helpdesk available 24/7 or offering the option to delay an antivirus scan until a more convenient time for the business user.

We will discuss additional recommendations from Chapter 9 onwards. But before we do that, let's take a look at how security managers perceive this problem.

CHAPTER 7: HOW SECURITY MANAGERS MAKE DECISIONS

Previous case studies demonstrate that security professionals often fail to consider how the policies they put in place could affect the day-to-day activities of employees in their companies.

First, we need to understand whether security managers perceive this as a problem. To explore this further, a number of interviews were conducted with security managers of major UK-based firms.

All of the information security experts selected to participate in the study had seven or more years of work experience in the field of information security and were holding managerial positions in their companies at the time of the interview.

The following insights from security managers were gathered as part of research at University College London.[17] Answers were anonymised to preserve the privacy of the individuals.

The main goal of these interviews was to gather insight into information security managers' awareness of the fact that decisions regarding the particular implementation of security controls affect organisations as a whole, and that their actions may negatively impact users' performance.

---

[17] Leron Zinatullin, "Modelling Conflicts between Security Compliance and Human Behaviour", dissertation, University College London, 2013.

The findings confirm that security managers mostly use their own judgement and past experience when making a decision regarding the implementation of particular information security controls.

"When I'm making a decision to implement some aspect of the ISO 27001 standard in my organisation," one security manager stated, "much of the decision centres on what the particular implementation would actually look like. ISO 27001 is very high-level and is by all means not a policy in itself – it just gives you one or two criteria or one or two suggestions as to how your security policies should look. As a result of the freedom of implementation, you actually have to write the policies yourself."

Security managers also understand the role of involving business management in the process of implementing security controls.

"If there is no benefit to the business, you don't do it," another expert mentioned, "You should start with the business – find the people who these controls directly affect and get their buy-in."

A common theme throughout was that business objectives should always be the priority. "Many security managers think that security is the most important thing. I personally don't think so," one manager admitted. "Paying shareholders is more important. Inhibiting those activities or encouraging dangerous activities because of what you are doing makes the situation worse."

There is also awareness among security managers of how to detect non-compliance in their organisations. "I walk around the building on occasion," one expert mentioned, "I wiggle doors and I check workstations for locked screens. The other way to gain insight into compliance is through rumours or chatting with people."

Most interviewed security managers agree that one should not punish users for non-compliance reflexively. One has to first understand the root cause of the problem. For instance, one expert suggested, "You don't react to non-compliance with anger, you try to find out why it happened, rather than just the fact that it has failed. Moreover, you use it as a possible trigger for education and awareness and possibility for improvement."

Another expert reinforces this point of view: "At the end of the day it failed because with high probability, you implemented it badly, because you forced some particular way of working or method which your employees can't use, so they worked around it."

Another common theme was that information security managers are, to a certain degree, aware of the impact of the security policy on users' behaviour. "Yes, I think I'm aware of the impact of my policies," one security manager said, "because when it affects users in a negative way, we hear about it. There are lots of complaints."

A number of information security managers backed up their statements with examples: "Some users want to look at a spreadsheet or use an application on their tablets but can't, because security controls don't allow access to the business applications via a tablet. So they have to use a laptop rather than a device of their own choice, and they are unhappy. So yes, we are aware of such tension."

These interview results suggest that this awareness is directly related to the number of user complaints.

Several security managers stated that it is difficult to assess the impact of security controls on user behaviour: "We never measured it," one manager admitted, "we don't have a way of measuring it. So we don't know."

This view was echoed: "It is one thing to put controls in place and another to measure effectiveness. When it comes to users it is very difficult. They are not like servers, where you can look at, for example, CPU performance before and after some change."

A subsequent theme emerged that focused on whether security managers are aware of the employees' daily business activities. It appears that they are, but only to the degree required in order to successfully manage their security projects.

"At a high level we are aware," one security manager said; "at the detailed process level really only when we are doing a project in that department, when we need to understand the processes within our project."

Another example that supports the same argument was brought up: "There are situations where we do a particular project on a new system. For example, if we are working on a new credit card system which is being implemented, we work through the users' roles and we work through the general data storage, so we become familiar with the supporting department's user activities."

The results illustrate that several participants believe they are capable of understanding users' day-to-day business activities and that they implement security controls accordingly.

All of the interviewed managers agreed that knowledge of what users in their company are doing can help them to improve the implementation of information security policies. One security manager stated, "For instance, we worked with our studio manager and looked at the process of data transfer to the client. We chose one particular brand of encrypted USB keys, and believed that adoption would be very high, because they are great-looking devices. It feels good for our creative workers to give this type of drive to the client, rather than sharing data using a cheap plastic USB stick – there is no story, there is no sort of emotional attachment, which is so particularly important for creative workers. But in order for us to come up with such a decision we actually spend some time observing and understanding our users."

This resulted in employees using secure, encrypted devices to transfer potentially confidential information rather than their own unencrypted drives.

The majority of security managers understand the importance of involving the user and assessing the possible impact on their behaviour when deciding how to implement particular security controls. However, they also agree that their awareness of users' business activities is reactive and based mainly on complaints.

We've heard from security managers, but the analysis is not complete until we have compared these views to those of the end-users themselves, in the next chapter.

CHAPTER 8: HOW USERS MAKE DECISIONS

It is not easy to gain insight into employee behaviour without contributions from people who are willing and able to honestly share their opinion on information security issues.

Kirlappos, Beautement and Sasse,[18] as part of their research, managed to build strong relationships with a number of organisations in the telecommunications and energy sectors who readily allowed access to their employees for the purposes of studying their compliance behaviour. The employees were assured that no sanctions would be imposed as a result of their participation.

The researchers conducted a series of interviews and identified three common reasons for non-compliance, which include those shown in Figure 8.

---

[18] Iacovos Kirlappos, Adam Beautement and M. Angela Sasse, "'Comply or Die' Is Dead: Long Live Security-Aware Principal Agents", in *Financial Cryptography and Data Security*, Springer, 2013, 70–82.

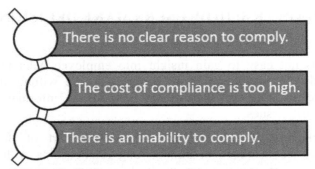

Figure 8: Common reasons for non-compliance

Let's examine each reason in more detail.

There is no clear reason to comply

The research results revealed that employees usually don't have an accurate concept of what information security is and what it aims to protect. They tend to lack a clear understanding of what certain security policies forbid and allow, which often leads to the creation of security myths. Even in those rare cases where employees are aware of a security policy and interpret it correctly, the motivation to comply is still lacking.

Non-security professionals are unlikely to be aware of the impact of their behaviour or to understand the associated risks. However, because following a policy involves a certain amount of effort, and if there is no immediate threat, non-compliant behaviour can appear to be the more attractive and comfortable option.

The study reveals typical examples of unintentional non-compliant behaviour. For example, employees seldom consider that deleted data can easily be recovered from drives that have been lost or stolen. They lack awareness that deleting data after completing a file transfer does not provide adequate protection. Furthermore, it is widely believed that the data stored on company laptops is secure because a password is required to gain access, but they are unaware that the data is unencrypted and can easily be retrieved from the hard drive. This leads to the insecure practice of storing sensitive data locally on laptops when travelling on public transport. What is also largely overlooked is that employees rarely consider that their actions might enable malware to enter their organisation's systems through the use of their personal USB sticks.

The cost of compliance is too high

The majority of employees within an organisation are hired to execute specific jobs, such as marketing, managing projects, manufacturing goods or overseeing financial investment. Their main, sometimes only, priority will be efficient completion of their core business activity, therefore information security will usually only be a secondary consideration. Consequently, employees will be reluctant to invest more than a limited amount of effort and time on such a secondary task which they rarely understand, and from which they perceive no benefit.

The findings suggest that when security mechanisms cause additional workload, employees will favour non-compliant behaviour in order to complete their primary tasks quickly.

There is a lack of awareness among security managers about the burden which security mechanisms impose on employees, because it is assumed that the users can easily accommodate the effort that security compliance requires. In reality, employees tend to experience a negative impact on their performance because they feel that these cumbersome security mechanisms drain both their time and their effort. The risk mitigation achieved through compliance, from their perspective, is not worth the disruption to their productivity. In extreme cases, the more urgent the delivery of the primary task is, the more appealing and justifiable non-compliance becomes, regardless of employees being aware of the risks.

When security mechanisms hinder or significantly slow down employees' performance, they will cut corners, and reorganise and adjust their primary tasks, in order to avoid them. This seems to be particularly prevalent in file sharing, especially when users are restricted by permissions, by data storage or transfer allowance, and by time-consuming protocols. People will usually work around the security mechanisms and resort to the readily available commercial alternatives, which may be insecure. From the employee's perspective, the consequences of not completing a primary task are severe, as opposed to the consequences of the "potential" risk associated with breaching security policies.

There is an inability to comply

There are extreme cases in which enforced compliance fails to be an option for employees, even when they are more than willing to invest their time and effort. In such cases, the predominant scenario is that users cannot comply because the security mechanisms do not match their basic requirements.

Examples include an organisation giving employees encrypted USB drives with too little storage space, forcing them to share files via email or via larger, non-encrypted drives. It is also common to see users copying files onto laptops because remote accessibility is problematic, or because their network drive capacity is too small.

Another recurring issue is a requirement for numerous passwords to access different corporate systems, all of which employees tend to have difficulty in memorising. Users will "fix" this problem by writing down their passwords, either physically on a document they carry with them or in an electronic form on their laptop.

People tend to be aware of how their behaviour can pose an increased risk, but feel justified in finding these workarounds because the organisation has failed to provide them with a proper technical implementation. They assume that the organisation would rather allow security violations than stop the main business process: an opinion that also happens to be adopted by managerial staff. When everybody shares this inadequate and risky perspective, the organisation is an accomplice in the employees' non-compliant behaviour.

The researchers concluded that implementation of security compliance seems to create a strain and enlarges the gap between security professionals and the rest of the organisation. Employees tend to develop a negative view of information security in general and respond to security enforcers with scepticism, or may simply ignore them.

This bias can easily discourage employees from behaving in a compliant manner with security controls, regardless of how sensibly designed they may be.

Overly complicated security mechanisms are usually implemented at the cost of the organisation's productivity, because they tend to consume valuable employee resources. It is not unusual to find that important parts of the organisation will foster non-compliant behaviour, because they value productivity over security and don't perceive any immediate risk.

Employees generally try to comply with an organisation's security policies, but, most importantly, they simply want to get their work done. Sometimes employees may violate an organisation's security policy through malicious behaviour, but it is often because of poor control implementation which does not consider their needs.

Here is where information security professionals' job gets interesting. When non-compliant behaviour is identified, they should first rule out the possibility of malicious behaviour, and then should understand where and why the security policy failed to work properly, forcing the employees to find workarounds.

The more a security policy implementation facilitates employee values and priorities, the better it fosters employee incentives and strengthens the security culture.

In order to achieve alignment between security and employee perspective, the process of formulating security policies must be focused on employee behaviour. A security professional should remember that employee performance is goal-oriented.

These goals are usually focused on business processes and their demands, and are generally seen as completely independent of information security goals, which are often perceived as abstract and lacking context.

When the viewpoint of employees is not taken into account, the end result is their partial or total absence as a factor in the process of designing security mechanisms. This often leads to, or enhances, the vicious cycle of developing an inadequate security culture, which in turn reinforces the misguided perception of security and the non-compliant behaviour that comes with it. In this scenario, security mechanisms can be considered to have a direct negative impact on employees' routine jobs. Successful engineering processes require the participation of key stakeholders involved.

The common reasons for non-compliant behaviour mentioned in this chapter serve as a good starting point and must be explored further and in detail within any given enterprise. They are at the very core of security design and must be common knowledge for security designers and policymakers.

CHAPTER 9: SECURITY AND USABILITY

In the previous chapter we mentioned that one of the main contributing factors to non-compliance by users is an extensive workload caused by poorly designed and poorly implemented security mechanisms. Next, we will discuss how these issues can be addressed.

Firstly, security professionals should understand that people's resources are limited. Moreover, people tend to struggle with making effective decisions when they are tired.

To test the validity of this argument, Shiv and Fedorikhin designed an experiment where they divided participants into two groups: the first group was asked to memorise a two-digit number (e.g. 54) and the second group was asked to remember a longer seven-digit number (e.g. 4509672).[19] They then asked the participants to go down the hall to the other room to collect their reward for participating. This payment, however, could only be received if the number was recalled correctly.

While they were making their way through the corridor, they encountered another experimenter, who offered them either fruit or the less healthy chocolate option. They were told that they could collect their chosen option after they

---

[19] Baba Shiv and Alexander Fedorikhin, "Heart and Mind in Conflict: The Interplay of Affect and Cognition in Consumer Decision Making", *Journal of Consumer Research*, 1999, 278–292.

finish the experiment, but they have to make a decision here and now.

The results demonstrated that people who were given the easier task of remembering a two-digit number mostly chose the healthy option, while people overburdened by the more challenging task of recalling a longer string of digits succumbed to the more gratifying chocolate.

The implications of these findings, however, are not only limited to dieting. A study conducted by Danzigera, Levav and Avnaim-Pessoa looks at the decision-making patterns that can be observed in the behaviour of judges when considering inmates for parole during different stages of the day.[20]

Despite rejecting parole being the default decision, in the mornings and after lunch judges had more cognitive capacity and energy to fully consider the details of the case and make an informed decision, resulting in more frequently granted paroles. In the evenings, judges tended to reject parole far more frequently, which is believed to be due to the mental strain they endure throughout the day. They simply ran out of energy and defaulted to the safest option.

How can this be applied to the information security context? Security professionals should bear in mind that if people are stressed at work, making difficult decisions, performing productive tasks, they get tired. This might affect their ability or willingness to maintain compliance.

---

[20] Shai Danziger, Jonathan Levav and Liora Avnaim-Pesso, "Extraneous Factors in Judicial Decisions", *Proceedings of the National Academy of Sciences*, 108(17), 2011, 6889–6892.

In a corporate context, this cognitive depletion may result in staff defaulting to core business activities at the expense of secondary security tasks, making the scenarios described in Chapter 6 a real possibility.

Let's look at the opportunities available to prevent such depletion.

When users perform tasks that comply with their own mental models (i.e. the natural way that they view the world and how they expect it to work), the activities present less of a cognitive challenge than those that work against said models.

If people can apply their previous knowledge and experience to a problem, less energy is required to solve it in a secure manner and they are less mentally depleted by the end of the day.

For example, a piece of research on disk sanitisation highlighted the importance of secure file removal from the hard disk.[21] It is not clear to users that emptying the "Recycle Bin" is insufficient and that files can easily be recovered. However, there are software products available which exploit the users' mental models from the physical world. They employ a "shredding" analogy to indicate that files are being removed securely, which echoes an activity they would perform at work. Such interface design might help lighten the burden on users.

---

[21] Simson L. Garfinkel and Abhi Shelat, "Remembrance of Data Passed: A Study of Disk Sanitization Practices", *IEEE Security & Privacy*, 1, 2003, 17–27.

Therefore security professionals should pay attention to the usability of security mechanisms, aligning them with the users existing mental models.

John Maeda supports the importance of relating to an existing experience to make design more user-friendly in *The Laws of Simplicity*.[22] He refers to an example of the desktop metaphor introduced by Xerox researchers in the 1980s. People were able to relate to the graphical computer interface as opposed to the command line. They could manipulate objects similarly to the way they do with the physical desk: store and categorise files in folders as well as move, rename or delete by placing them in the recycle bin.

Building on existing mental models makes the adoption of new technologies and ways of working easier. However, such mappings must take cultural background into consideration. The metaphor might not work if it is not part of the existing mental model. For instance, Apple Macintosh's original trash icon was impossible to recognise in Japan, where users were not accustomed to metallic bins of this kind.

Good interface design not only lightens the burden on users but can also complement security. Traditionally, it has been assumed that security and usability always contradict each other – that security makes things more complicated, while usability aims to improve the user experience. In reality, they can support each other by defining constructive and destructive activities. Effective

---

[22] John Maeda, *The Laws of Simplicity*, MIT Press, 2006.

design should make constructive activities simple to perform while hindering destructive ones.

This can be achieved by incorporating security activities into the natural workflow of productive tasks, which requires the involvement of security professionals early in the design process. Security and usability shouldn't be extra features introduced as an afterthought once the system has been developed, but an integral part of the design from the beginning.

Security professionals can provide input into the design process via several methods such as iterative or participatory design.[23] The iterative method consists of each development cycle being followed by testing and evaluation and the participatory method ensures that key stakeholders, including security professionals, have an opportunity to be involved.

Including security requirements from the very start is not necessarily enough to guarantee the success of solving a particular security-usability issue. The reason for this is that such problems can be categorised as *wicked*.

Rittel and Webber define a wicked problem in the context of social policy planning as a challenging, if not impossible, one to solve due to missing, poorly defined or inconsistent requirements from stakeholders, which may

---

[23] For iterative design see J. Nielsen, "Iterative User Interface Design", *IEEE Computer*, 26(11) (1993), 32–41; for participatory design see D. Schuler and A. Namioka, *Participatory Design: Principles and Practices*, CRC Press, 1993.

morph over time and which can be demanding to find an optimal solution for.[24]

Therefore one cannot apply traditional methods to solving a wicked problem; a creative solution must be sought instead. One of these creative solutions could be to apply *design thinking* techniques.

Methods for design thinking include performing situational analysis, interviewing, creating user profiles, looking at other existing solutions, creating prototypes and mind mapping.

Plattner, Meinel and Leifer assert that there are four rules to design thinking, which can help security professionals better approach wicked problems:[25]

1. The human rule: all design activity is ultimately social in nature.
2. The ambiguity rule: design thinkers must preserve ambiguity.
3. The redesign rule: all design is redesign
4. The tangibility rule: making ideas tangible always facilitates communication.

Security professionals should adopt these rules in order to develop secure and usable controls, by engaging people, utilising existing solutions and creating prototypes which can help, by allowing the collection of feedback.

---

[24] Horst W. J. Rittel and Melvin M. Webber, "Dilemmas in a General Theory of Planning", *Policy Sciences*, 4, 1973, 155–169.

[25] Hasso Plattner, Christoph Meinel and Larry J. Leifer, eds., *Design Thinking: Understand–Improve–Apply*, Springer Science & Business Media, 2010.

9: Security and Usability

Although this enables the design of better security controls, the design thinking rules rarely provide an insight on why the existing mechanism is failing.

When a problem occurs, we naturally tend to focus on the symptoms instead of identifying the root cause. Taiichi Ohno developed the Five Whys technique, which was used in the Toyota production system as a systematic problem-solving tool to get to the heart of the problem.

In one of his books, Ohno provides the following example of applying this technique when a machine stopped functioning:[26]

1. Why did the machine stop? There was an overload and the fuse blew
2. Why was there an overload? The bearing was not sufficiently lubricated.
3. Why was it not lubricated sufficiently? The lubrication pump was not pumping sufficiently
4. Why was it not pumping sufficiently? The shaft of the pump was worn and rattling
5. Why was the shaft worn out? There was no strainer attached and metal scrap got in.

Instead of focusing on resolving the first reason for the malfunction, i.e. replacing the fuse or the pump shaft, repeating "why" five times can help to uncover the underlying issue and prevent the problem from resurfacing again in the near future.

---

[26] Taiichi Ohno, *Toyota Production System: Beyond Large-Scale Production*, Productivity Press, 1988.

Eric Reis, who adapted this technique to starting up a business in his book *The Lean Startup*,[27] points out that at "the root of every seemingly technical problem is actually a human problem."

As in Ohno's example, the root cause turned out to be human error (an employee forgetting to attach a strainer), rather than a technical fault (a blown fuse), as was initially suspected. This is typical of most problems that security professionals face, no matter which industry they are in.

These techniques can help to address the core of the issue and build systems that are both usable and secure. This is not easy to achieve due to the nature of the problem. But once implemented, such mechanisms can significantly improve the security culture in organisations.

---

[27] Eric Reis, *The Lean Startup*, Crown Business, 2011.

CHAPTER 10: SECURITY CULTURE

Demonstrating to employees that security is there to make their life easier, not harder, is the first step in developing a sound security culture in a company. But before we discuss the actual steps to improve it, let's first understand the root causes of poor security culture.

Security professionals must understand that bad habits and behaviours tend to be contagious. Malcolm Gladwell, in his book *The Tipping Point*,[28] discusses the conditions which allow some ideas or behaviours to "spread like viruses". He refers to the *broken windows theory* to illustrate the power of context. The theory was first presented by Wilson and Kelling,[29] who advocated for stopping smaller crimes by maintaining the environment in order to prevent bigger ones. The authors claim that a broken window left for several days in a neighbourhood would trigger more vandalism. The small defect signals a lack of care and attention on the property, which in turn implies that crime will go unpunished.

Gladwell describes the efforts of George Kelling, who employed the theory to fight vandalism on the New York City subway system. He argued that cleaning up graffiti on the trains would prevent further vandalism. Gladwell

---

[28] Malcolm Gladwell, *The Tipping Point: How Little Things Can Make a Big Difference*, Little, Brown, 2006.
[29] James Q. Wilson and George L. Kelling, "Broken Windows: The Police and Neighborhood Safety", *The Atlantic*, 29(31), 1982, 29–38.

concluded that this several-year-long effort resulted in a dramatically reduced crime rate.

Despite ongoing debate regarding the causes of the 1990s crime rate reduction in the US, the broken windows theory can be applied in an information security context.

Security professionals should remember that minor policy violations tend to lead to bigger ones, eroding the security culture of the firm.

We discussed the reasons for violations in Chapter 8, but there is more to it than that. The psychology of human behaviour should be considered as well. Sometimes people are not motivated to comply with a security policy because they simply don't see the financial impact of violating it.

Dan Ariely, in his book *The Honest Truth about Dishonesty*,[30] tries to understand why people break the rules. Among other experiments, he describes a survey conducted among golf players to determine the conditions in which they would be tempted to move the ball into a more advantageous position, and if so, which method they would choose. The golfers were offered three different options: they could use their club, use their shoe or simply pick the ball up using their hands.

Although all of these options break the rules, they were designed in this way to determine if one method of cheating is more psychologically acceptable than others. The results of the study demonstrated that moving the ball

---

[30] Dan Ariely, *The Honest Truth about Dishonesty*, Harper, 2013.

with a club was the most common choice, followed by the shoe and, finally, the hand. It turned out that physically and psychologically distancing ourselves from the "immoral" action makes people more likely to act dishonestly.

It is important to understand that the "distance" described in this experiment is merely psychological. It doesn't change the nature of the action.

In a security context, employees in a company will usually be reluctant to steal confidential information, just as golfers will refrain from picking up a ball with their hand to move it to a more favourable position, because that way they are directly involved in the unethical behaviour. However, employees might download a peer-to-peer sharing software to listen to music while at work, as the impact of this action is less obvious. This can potentially lead to even bigger losses due to even more confidential information being stolen from the corporate network.

Security professionals can use this finding to remind employees of the true meaning of their actions. Breaking security policy does not seem to have a direct financial impact on the company – there is usually no perceived loss; hence it is easy for employees to engage in such behaviour. Highlighting this link and demonstrating the correlation between policy violations and the ability of the business to generate revenue could help employees to understand the consequences of non-compliance.

Building upon the connection between breaking security policies and cheating, let's look at another study conducted by Gino, Ayal and Ariely,[31] where they asked participants to solve 20 simple maths problems and promised 50 cents for each correct answer.

The participants were allowed to check their own answers and then shred the answer sheet, leaving no evidence of any potential cheating. The results demonstrated that participants reported to solve, on average, five more problems than under conditions where cheating was not possible (i.e. controlled conditions).

The researchers then introduced David – a student who was tasked to raise his hand shortly after the experiment begun and proclaim that he had solved all the problems. Other participants were obviously shocked by such a statement. It was clearly impossible to solve all the problems in only a few minutes. The experimenter, however, didn't question his integrity and suggested that David should shred the answer sheet and take all the money from the envelope.

Interestingly, other participants' behaviour adapted as a result. They reported solving on average eight more problems than under controlled conditions.

Much like the broken windows theory, this demonstrates that unethical behaviour is contagious, as are acts of non-compliance. If employees in a company witness other people breaking security policies and not being punished, they are tempted to do the same. It becomes socially

---

[31] Francesca Gino, Shahar Ayal and Dan Ariely, "Contagion and Differentiation in Unethical Behavior: The Effect of One Bad Apple on the Barrel", *Psychological Science*, 20(3), 2009, 393–398.

acceptable and normal. This is the root cause of poor security culture.

The good news is that the opposite holds true as well. That's why security culture has to have strong senior management support. Leading by example is the key to changing the perception of security in the company: if employees see that the leadership team takes security seriously, they will follow.

Therefore security professionals should focus on how security is perceived. Brooks supports this point, outlining three basic steps in decision-making in his book *The Social Animal*:[32]

1. People perceive a situation.
2. People estimate if the action is in their long-term interest.
3. People use willpower to take action.

Figure 9: Basic steps of decision-making

He claims that people historically were mostly focused on the last two steps of this process. We have demonstrated in the previous chapter that relying solely on willpower only has a limited effect. Willpower can be exercised like a muscle, but it is also prone to atrophy.

---

[32] David Brooks, *The Social Animal: The Hidden Sources of Love, Character, and Achievement*, Random House, 2011.

In regard to the second step of the decision-making process, if people were reminded of the potential negative consequences they would be likely not to take the action. Brooks then refers to ineffective HIV/AIDS awareness campaigns, which focused only on the negative consequences, but ultimately failed to change people's behaviour.

He also suggests that most diets fail because willpower and reason are not strong enough to confront impulsive desires. "You can tell people not to eat the French fry. You can give them pamphlets about the risks of obesity … In their nonhungry state, most people will vow not to eat it. But when their hungry self rises, their well-intentioned self fades, and they eat the French fry".

This doesn't only apply to dieting. As demonstrated in Chapter 6, when people want to get their job done and security gets in the way, they will circumvent it, regardless of the degree of risk they might expose the company to.

That is the reason for perception being the cornerstone of the decision-making process. Employees have to be taught to see security violations in a particular way that minimises the temptation to break policies.

Timothy Wilson claims, "One of the most enduring lessons of social psychology is that behaviour change often precedes changes in attitudes and feelings".[33]

---

[33] Timothy Wilson, *Strangers to Ourselves*, Harvard University Press, 2004, 212.

Security professionals should understand that there is no single event that alters users' behaviour – changing security culture requires regular reinforcement, creating and sustaining habits.

Charles Duhigg, in his book *The Power of Habit*,[34] tells a story about Paul O'Neill, a CEO of the Aluminium Company of America (Alcoa) who was determined to make his enterprise the safest in the country. At first people were confused that the newly appointed executive was not talking about profit margins or other finance-related metrics. They didn't see the link between his "zero-injuries" goal and the company's performance. Despite that, Alcoa's profits reached a historical high within a year of his announcement. When O'Neill retired, the company's annual income was five times greater than it had been before his arrival. Moreover, it became one of the safest companies in the world.

Duhigg explains this phenomenon by highlighting the importance of the "keystone habit". Alcoa's CEO identified safety as such a habit and focused solely on it.

O'Neill had a challenging goal to transform the company, but he couldn't just tell people to change their behaviour. He said, "that's not how the brain works. So I decided I was going to start by focusing on one thing. If I could start disrupting the habits around one thing, it would spread throughout the entire company."

He recalled an incident when one of his workers died trying to fix a machine despite the safety procedures and

---

[34] Charles Duhigg, *The Power of Habit: Why We Do What We Do and How to Change*, Random House, 2013.

warning signs. The CEO called an emergency meeting to understand what had caused this tragic event.

He took personal responsibility for the worker's death, identifying numerous shortcomings in safety education. For example, the training programme didn't highlight the fact that employees wouldn't be blamed for machinery failure or the fact that they shouldn't commence repair work before finding a manager.

As a result, the policies were updated and the employees were encouraged to suggest safety improvements. Workers, however, went a step further and started suggesting business improvements as well. Changing their behaviour around safety led to some innovative solutions, enhanced communication and overall increased profits for the company.

Security professionals should understand the importance of group dynamics and influences to build an effective security culture.

They should also remember that just as "broken windows" encourages policy violations, changing one security habit can encourage better behaviour across the board.

Improving security culture, however, is difficult without a better understanding of the human decision-making process, so let's look at this in more detail in the next chapter.

CHAPTER 11: THE PSYCHOLOGY OF COMPLIANCE

The human decision-making process is the preferred subject of psychologists and economists. Historically, they adopted an approach of viewing human behaviour as regular and highly predictable. This helped the researchers to build various models in order to comprehend social and economical phenomena. Such systems were compared by Karl Popper to reliable pendulum clocks.[35] One can take them apart and observe how the pieces fit together. People, however, are much more complicated. Their behaviour, which is considered to be "highly irregular and disorderly," has more in common with clouds, which are harder to predict due to their dynamic and constantly changing nature. Various theories were later developed to understand the drivers underlying certain actions. Such findings have been adopted by information security researchers to understand human behaviour in relation to policy compliance.

One of the dominant theories pertaining to human behaviour is the *theory of rational choice*. This theory provides insight into social and economic behaviour, and reveals how people aim to maximise their personal benefits and minimise their costs; personal gain tends to

---

[35] Karl Raimund Popper, "Of Clocks and Clouds: An Approach to the Problem of Rationality and the Freedom of Man," in *Objective Knowledge: An Evolutionary Approach*, Clarendon Press, 1972, 206–265.

.

be the main motivator. People make decisions based on the perceived benefit as well as the cost of the outcome, and act accordingly.

This theory can also be used to explain how employees make decisions about whether or not to comply with a particular information security policy. According to this theory, it might be rational for users not to comply with a security policy, because the effort outweighs the perceived level of risk reduction.

Aytes and Connolly,[36] for example, observed frequent unsafe computer-related practices among university students, which included revealing passwords, downloading attachments without running an antivirus scan and not backing up their data, among other things.

Their findings show that although the students were quite familiar with safe computing behaviour, they still continued to exhibit risky conduct.

They conclude that organisations may have to go a step further than simply recommending safe computing behaviour: they suggest that compliance may have to be imposed by more forceful means.

I interviewed Daniel Schatz, Director for Threat and Vulnerability Management at Thomson Reuters, to understand his view on this subject. He believes that inconvenience is the main driver for users' non-compliant behaviour: "Everyone is unconsciously and constantly

---

[36] Kregg Aytes and Terry Connolly, "Computer and Risky Computing Practices: A Rational Choice Perspective", *Journal of Organizational End User Computing*, 16(2), 2004, 22–40.

doing a cost–benefit calculation; if a users' expected utility of opening the 'Cute Bunnies' attachment exceeds the inconvenience of ignoring all those warning messages, a reasonable decision was made, albeit an insecure one."

The solution might be to either raise the cost or lower the benefit of non-compliance. While it will be difficult to teach the staff to dislike cute bunnies, raising the cost may succeed.

"To stick with the previous example, this could be done by imposing punishment for opening malicious attachments or deploying technology solutions to aid the user in being compliant."

There is an operational and economic perspective to this, of course. If employees are scared to open attachments because of the potential for punishment, it may tarnish the reputation of the security function.

"Some will probably look for 'security awareness training' as an answer here; while there is a place for such training, the impact of it is low. If security awareness training aims to change an organisation's culture, you're on the right track, but trying to train users' utility-based decisions away will fail".

To explore whether the punishment suggested by Schatz can indeed be effective, let's look into the *theory of general deterrence.*

This theory suggests that users will not comply with the rules if they know that breaking them will not be followed by punishment. Before elaborating on this theory, it is worth defining the terms *intrinsic motivation* and *extrinsic motivation*. Intrinsic motivation comes from within the individual, which usually leads to engaging in behaviour that is personally rewarding. In this context, people are not driven by the idea of an external incentive, rather by their own desires. Extrinsic motivation, on the other hand, results from the hope of gaining an external reward or avoiding punishment for specific conduct.

Extrinsic	Intrinsic
• Rewards • Fear of punishment • Competition	• Meaning • Enjoyment • Interest

Figure 10: Extrinsic vs. intrinsic motivation factors

D'Arcy, Hovav and Galletta refer to an extended version of the theory of general deterrence to find out if information security awareness training affects the perception of company sanctions in terms of severity and certainty.[37] They collected a sample of 269 employees from eight different companies who had received such training and were aware of the presence of user-monitoring software on their machines. Their findings show that the perception of sanctions is more effective in deterring risky behaviour than imposing actual sanctions.

---

[37] John D'Arcy, Anat Hovav and Dennis Galletta, "User Awareness of Security Countermeasures and Its Impact on Information Systems Misuse: A Deterrence Approach", *Information Systems Research*, 17(1), 2009, 79–98.

Jai-Yeol challenged the significance of these findings, which use the theory of general deterrence to deal with and predict behaviour related to compliance, because the approaches that are postulated are solely based on extrinsic motivation.[38] The author states that this model lacks the consideration of intrinsic motivation, which is an important aspect and strong driving force of the human character. He proposes a model including both the intrinsic and extrinsic motivators of human behaviour. Analysis of a sample of 602 employees revealed that approaches relating to the intrinsic motivation paradigm led to a significant increase in compliant employee behaviour over approaches relating to the extrinsic motivation model.

Another theory – the *cognitive evaluation theory* – supports the importance of intrinsic motivation. It can be used to predict the effects that rewards have on intrinsic motivation, specifically when these rewards are of a tangible nature, such as awards and prizes, as opposed to verbal rewards or recognition.

Following this theory, when rewards are perceived as a means of controlling behaviour, they have a negative effect on intrinsic motivation. A recipient's sense of autonomy and self-determination will decline when they feel that they are being controlled.

Additionally, the cognitive evaluation theory also explains why verbal or non-tangible rewards have positive effects

---

[38] Jai-Yeol Son, "Out of Fear or Desire? Toward a Better Understanding of Employees' Motivation to Follow IS Security Policies", *Information &. Management*, 48(7), 2011, 296–302.

on intrinsic motivation. In order for employees to feel increasingly like they are skilful at completing certain tasks and that their performance has been positively evaluated by their supervisors, non-tangible rewards of this type must be delivered in a way that is not perceived as coercive. This type of reward system would boost employees' performance and determination as a result of increased intrinsic motivation.

Within an information security context, this theory recommends adoption of a positive, non-tangible reward system to attain constructive behaviour regarding security policy compliance.

All of the above theories suggest that to effectively protect companies' assets, the security professional should develop and implement security policies not only to ensure formal compliance with legal and regulatory requirements, but also to ensure that the motivations and attitudes of users are also considered.

Policies should be designed in a way that reduces the mental and physical workload of users by fostering intrinsic motivation, while reducing extrinsic motivation or deterrence. Security professionals and policymakers should keep the employee's perspectives in mind and at the very core of their approaches to designing security policies.

CHAPTER 12: CONCLUSION - CHANGING THE APPROACH TO SECURITY

In order to reduce security risks within an enterprise, security professionals have traditionally attempted to guide employee behaviour towards compliance by communicating the cost of risk and through security training. However, recurring problems and employee behaviour in this arena indicate that these measures are insufficient and rather ineffective.

Security training tends to focus on specific working practices and defined threat scenarios, leaving the understanding of security culture and its specific principles of behaviour untouched. A security culture should be regarded as a fundamental matter to address. If neglected, employees will not develop habitually secure behaviour or take the initiative to make better decisions when problems arise.

When information security solutions are created to fit into employees' day-to-day jobs, rates of compliance increase and a more positive outlook on security is attained, which will in turn result in a healthier, stronger and more objective security culture within the organisation.

If security professionals want to steer employee behaviour towards compliance, they must first shift their decision-making processes in the same direction. In order to do so, security professionals must have a look at their individual cost–benefit analyses. Security implementations must not only accommodate users' needs and priorities; they must also be an economically attractive option.

Kirlappos, Beautement and Sasse, in the research which we discussed in Chapter 8, identified four main factors that can help modify employee perception of the cost–benefit balance towards compliance. These include *design, culture, supervision* and *sanctioning*.

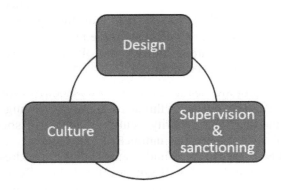

Figure 11: Factors which modify employee perception

Design

In order to minimise compliance costs, an organisation should make sure that all the mechanisms of security are functioning properly within a specific context. For example, the organisation could provide their employees with encrypted USB drives, as well as a network drive for saving their documents. Each one must have adequate storage capacity, so that they won't run out of space and have to seek alternative, insecure options for storing their work. Additionally, in order to enhance security, these network drives can be combined with auto-archiving systems that will prevent sensitive information from being transported within employee laptops when they travel. Risks can be reduced further by providing employees with encrypted laptop drives in case they have to store their documents locally, along with improved remote access which can diminish the need to transfer information across different channels. Moreover, employees would stop writing down passwords if they are using single sign-on systems.

Furthermore, an organisation should facilitate the conditions that will enable situational and local adjustments to these security mechanisms. For example, when an employee needs to access a blocked website, they are given the option to proceed with the knowledge that activity will be logged and reviewed at a later date by the security team to ensure that no malware was picked up.

This point focuses on the flexibility that employees may require to have access to certain systems in order to complete their primary tasks when they encounter a problem. Usually, when this occurs, they don't have the luxury of waiting for the authorised personnel to act and they will be forced to find workarounds to gain this access – they will normally resort to trusted work colleagues, as illustrated in Chapter 8.

The security mechanisms, processes and technology must be closely aligned with the needs of the employees and the demands of their primary tasks.

Culture

Once employees' primary tasks are identified and aligned with the security systems which enable compliance, the next step for an organisation to consider is to create awareness of information risks and teach the principles for managing them. The goal is not to teach tricks, but to create a new culture which is accepted and understood by everyone. In order to effectively do so, messages need to be designed and delivered according to each type of employee: there is no such thing as a one-size-fits-all security campaign. Questions that must always be answered include: What are the benefits? What does it matter or why should I care? What impact do my actions have?

Security campaigns must discard scare tactics such as threatening employees with sanctions for breaches. Campaigns should be oriented towards the users' goals and values, as well as the values of the organisation, such as professionalism and delivery.

A security campaign should emphasise that employees can cause serious damage to an organisation when they engage in non-compliant behaviour, even if it appears to be in an insignificant way. They should understand that they are bearing some responsibility for the security of the organisation and its exposure to risk.

Furthermore, the entire organisation needs to perceive security as bringing value to the company, as opposed to being an obstacle preventing employees from doing their job. It is important for employees to understand that they contribute to the smooth and efficient operation of business processes when they follow recommended security practices, just as security enables the availability of resources that support these processes.

Security campaigns that are group-targeted enable greater flexibility: the more an organisation's employees are adequately aware of the need for security, the easier it is to create behavioural change via education. When everybody is sufficiently aware of the vulnerabilities and threats inherent in their jobs, the organisation can apply an effective training programme by testing their knowledge, and then resort back to education whenever a misconception is found. From this point on, only role-specific reminders of the key messages are required to reinforce awareness and update employees on the latest risks and vulnerabilities. Additionally, educational material and user-friendly information should always be accessible to employees when they need a reference.

Supervision and sanctioning

Expensive architectural solutions – technical and physical mechanisms used to prevent unwanted behaviour – become obsolete once an organisation's security systems favour compliance and its employees are well informed regarding the security risks relating to their jobs. In this scenario, compliant behaviour comes directly from employees who are interested in behaving securely and not as a result of the obstacles or threats imposed upon them. Voluntary compliant behaviour is usually the result of standards that arise from the existence of both informal and formal rules within the organisation. This method is significantly cheaper and easier to enforce, as it usually results from and further breeds a positive atmosphere, in which employees feel that their organisation trusts them to perform within compliance and even promote it. It is considered that companies where employees have more responsibilities and feel trusted by their enterprise are more likely to establish a high level of security awareness and an improved understanding of the need for security. On the other hand, employees who don't feel trusted in a traditional command-and-control environment are easily demoralised and will rarely voluntarily engage in compliant behaviour.

However, if employees abuse trust, they should be punished. Supervision mechanisms should be implemented so that abuse of trust can be detected. When sanctions are enforced in such circumstances, employees are less likely to attempt further abuse of trust.

* * *

In this book we've discussed basic aspects of information security, including confidentiality, integrity and availability, and how they relate to vulnerabilities and threats.

We summarised this discussion by highlighting the importance of careful risk management and aligning the security programme with wider business objectives.

To achieve that, we talked about various methods and techniques to engage stakeholders and encourage buy-in, which is particularly important in the context of governance.

We looked at how security managers with good intentions implement security controls in a way which may negatively impact employee's productivity. We further analysed reasons for non-compliance from the end-users' perspective, acknowledging the mismatch against security managers' views.

If organisations continue to set equally high goals for both security and business productivity, they are essentially leaving it up to their employees to resolve potential conflicts between them. As we have seen, employees will focus most of their time and effort on carrying out their primary tasks efficiently and in a timely manner, which means that their target will be to maximise their own benefit, as opposed to the company's. It is therefore vital for organisations to find a balance between both security and productivity, because when they fail to do so, they lead – or even force – their employees to resort to non-compliant behaviour. When companies are unable to recognise and correct security mechanisms and policies that affect performance and when they exclusively reward their employees for productivity, not for security, they are effectively enabling and reinforcing non-compliant decision-making on behalf of the employees. Furthermore, companies seldom impose sanctions that are intended to be enacted in the case of non-compliant behaviour.

Employees will only comply with security policies if they are motivated to do so: they must have the perception that compliant behaviour results in personal gain. People must be given the tools and the means to understand the potential risks associated with their roles, as well as the benefits of compliant behaviour, both to themselves and to the organisation. Once they are equipped with this information and awareness, they must be trusted to make their own decisions that can serve to mitigate risks at the organisational level.

The traditional approach, whereby security experts "police" employee performance by defining the security mechanisms without taking business processes or individual tasks into account, clearly fails to work in modern, geographically distributed organisations that strive for agility and encourage individuals to take the initiative and make their ideas known. Many companies have evolved from compliance to risk-based information security frameworks, such as ISO 27001, but have not adapted their management of employees' security behaviour in an analogous way, which negatively influences employee compliance.

The rich diversity of the situational and local context, in which each employee makes a decision, cannot be effectively or reasonably covered by a one-size-fits-all approach. Flexibility and adaptability are essential mechanisms to use when conflicts between tasks and business processes arise.

Security mechanisms must be aligned with individual primary tasks in order to ensure effective implementation, by factoring in an individual's perspective, knowledge and awareness, and a modern, flexible and adaptable information security approach. The aim should therefore be to correct employee misunderstandings and misconceptions that result in non-compliant behaviour, because, in the end, people are a company's best asset.

APPENDIX: ANALOGIES

I'm passionate about helping people understand security. In my experience, using analogies is one of the best tools to enhance learning. People have a far better and longer-lasting understanding of a concept when they can relate to a real-life experience that emulates it. Describing situations and possible outcomes can be just as easily done by telling stories: they are not only pleasant to read, hear or imagine, but they also transfer knowledge in the most effective way.

That's why I decided to contribute to the Analogies Project.[39] The aim of this project is to illustrate the importance of information security in the modern world, by drawing parallels between what people already know and how these relate to information security.

In this appendix I would like to share a couple of my analogies to help you to communicate the value of security.

Analogy 1: Cake and Security

There is no doubt that security is necessary, but why is it so unpleasant to follow a security policy? Reminding yourself to stick to the rules feels like your partner telling you … to eat your salad. You know they are right, but anticipating that bland taste and mindless chewing that awaits you simply puts you off. You decide to leave it for tomorrow, so much so that you never get to it.

---

[39] See *https://theanalogiesproject.org/*.

Cakes, on the other hand, are yummy and require no effort whatsoever to indulge in our cravings for them. Nobody needs to force us to eat a piece.

In our day-to-day lives we prefer to do 'cake' tasks without giving it a second's thought. Things like storing confidential files on Dropbox or emailing them to our personal accounts ... you know, taking a little bite here and there. It's 'only for today', 'no biggie' ... This one-time thing is so harmless, it's like a comfort snack. We might later feel guilty that we bypassed a few 'salad' controls. Maybe we used our personal USB drive instead of a company-issued encrypted one, but at the end of the day ... who cares? Who will notice? As long as there is no dramatic impact on our health, a bite here or a bite there won't cause any harm.

And one day we realise that it's not all rosy. The result of our laziness or lack of willpower eventually rears its ugly head when the doctor makes us stand on the scales and has a look at our blood pressure. So to add to your partner's words of wisdom is the doctor's warning of an unhealthy present and a bleak future; something that would sound very similar during the company's security audit:

"You have got to eat more salad and lay off the cakes!"

To make matters worse, even with our best intentions to have the salad at the office cafeteria, we discover that the one available is practically inedible. Pretty much like finding that the company's secure shared drive doesn't have the necessary space to store our files or that the encrypted pen drive is not compatible with the client's Mac.

Appendix: Analogies

So if there are chefs coming up with ways to make salads more appealing, what can security professionals do to help us, the employees, maintain our 'security diet'?

They could aim at making security more like a cake – effortless, even attractive, but still keep it as healthy as a salad. Sound simple? Perhaps not so much, but they should invest in usability studies to make sure that the secure solution is the easiest to use. It might involve discovering an entirely new culinary art altogether: how to make a cake-tasting salad. But if they fail to realise just how unpalatable the salads are to begin with, we should let them know. Security professionals need employees' support.

Organisations are like families: everyone has to stay healthy, otherwise when a single member gets sick, the whole family is at risk of getting sick as well, whether it be catching an infectious disease or adopting an unhealthy lifestyle. It's like having the slimmest, fittest family member refrain from adding biscuits to the grocery list in order not to tempt the couch potatoes. It's a team effort. In order for a company to stay healthy, everyone has to keep a healthy lifestyle of eating salad regularly, even when it is not that pleasant.

The whole company needs to know that security is important for achieving its goals – not something that gets in the way – just as we should all know that having a healthy diet of greens will guarantee a sound body. Employees contribute to the efficient operation of the business when they comply with security policies. Not only does security ensure confidentiality and the integrity of information, but it also guarantees that the resources are available for employees to complete their primary tasks.

We need to realise that we contribute to security, and we can inflict serious damage on a company when we don't comply with security policies, no matter how insignificant or harmless they may seem. As employees, we are individually responsible for the organisation's exposure to security risks, just as we are responsible for exposing ourselves to illness. Our behaviour and daily regime significantly shape our quality of life, and our practices shape the quality of our business.

The health of the company is everyone's business. Let's all eat our salad while helping the security specialists to come up with better-tasting ones.

Analogy 2: Poker and Security

Good poker players are known to perform well under pressure. They play their cards based on rigorous probability analysis and impact assessment. These skills are very similar to those which a security professional must have for managing information security risks.

What can security professionals learn from a game of cards? It turns out, quite a bit. Skilled poker players are very good at making educated guesses about opponents' cards and predicting their next moves. Security professionals are also required to be on the forefront of emerging threats and discovered vulnerabilities to see what the attackers' next move might be.

At the beginning of a traditional Texas hold'em poker match, players are only dealt two cards (a hand). Based on this limited information, they have to try to evaluate the odds of winning, and act accordingly. Players can either decide to stay in the game – in this case they have to pay a fee which contributes to the overall pot – or give up (fold). Security professionals also usually make decisions under a high degree of uncertainty. There are many ways they can treat risk: they can mitigate it by implementing necessary controls, avoid, transfer or accept it. Costs of such decisions vary as well.

Not all cards, however, are worth playing. Similarly, not all security countermeasures should be implemented. Sometimes it is more effective to fold your cards and accept the risk than to pay for an expensive control. When the odds are right a security professional can start a project to implement a security change to increase the security posture of a company.

When the game progresses and the first round of betting is over, the players are presented with a new piece of information. The poker term 'flop' is used for the three additional cards that the dealer places on the table. These cards can be used to create a winning combination with each player's hand. When the cards are revealed, the player has the opportunity to reassess the situation and make a decision. This is exactly the way in which the changing market conditions or business requirements provide an instant to re-evaluate the business case for implementing a security countermeasure.

There is nothing wrong with terminating a security project. If a poker player had a strong hand in the beginning, but the flop shows that there is no point in continuing, it means that conditions have changed. Maybe engaging key stakeholders revealed that a certain risk is not that critical and that implementation costs might be too high. Feel free to pass. It is much better to cancel a security project than to end up with a solution that is ineffective and costly.

However, if poker players are sure that they are right, they have to be ready to defend their hand. In terms of security, it might mean convincing the board of the importance of the countermeasure based on rigorous cost–benefit analysis. Security professionals can still lose the game and the company might get breached, but at least they proactively did everything in their power to mitigate that.

It doesn't matter if poker players win or lose a particular hand as long as they make sound decisions that bring desired long-term results. Even the best poker player can't win every hand. Similarly, security professionals can't mitigate every security risk and implement all the possible countermeasures. To stay in the game, it is important to develop and follow a security strategy that will help to protect against ever-evolving threats in a cost-effective way.

SOURCES

Adams, A., and M. A. Sasse: "Users Are Not the Enemy: Why Users Compromise Security Mechanisms and How to Take Remedial Measures", *Communications of the ACM*, 42(12), December 1999, 40–46.

Adams, J, "Risk Management: It's Not Rocket Science … It's Much More Complicated", *Risk Management*, 54(5) 2007, 36–40.

Albrechtsen, E., and J. Hovden, "The Information Security Digital Divide between Information Security Managers and Users", *Computers & Security*, 28(6), 2009 476–490.

Anttila, J., and J. Kajava, "Challenging IS and ISM Standardization for Business Benefits", paper delivered at ARES '10 International Conference on Availability, Reliability, and Security, 2010.

Ariely, D., *The Honest Truth about Dishonesty*, Harper, 2013.

Aytes, K., and T. Connolly, "Computer and Risky Computing Practices: A Rational Choice Perspective", *Journal of Organizational End User Computing* 16(2), 2004, 22–40.

Bartsch, S., and M. A. Sasse, "Guiding Decisions on Authorization Policies: A Participatory Approach to Decision Support", in ACM SAC 2012, Trento, Italy, 2012.

Sources

Bartsch, S., and M. A. Sasse, "How Users Bypass Access Control and Why: The Impact of Authorization Problems on Individuals and the Organization", ECIS2013: The 21st European Conference in Information Systems, 2013, in press.

Beautement, A., M. A. Sasse and M. Wonham, "The Compliance Budget: Managing Security Behaviour in Organisations", in NSPW '08: Proceedings of the 2008 Workshop on New Security Paradigms, 47–58.

Björck, F., "Security Scandinavian Style", PhD dissertation, Stockholm University, 2001.

Brooks, D., *The Social Animal: The Hidden Sources of Love, Character, and Achievement*, Random House, 2011.

Bulgurcu, B., H. Cavusoglu and I. Benbasat, "Information Security Policy Compliance: An Empirical Study of Rationality-Based Beliefs and Information Security Awareness", *MIS Quarterly*, 34(3), 2010, 523–548.

Danziger, S., J. Levav and L. Avnaim-Pesso, "Extraneous Factors in Judicial Decisions", *Proceedings of the National Academy of Sciences*, 108(17), 2011, 6889–6892.

D'Arcy, J., A. Hovav and D. Galletta, "User Awareness of Security Countermeasures and Its Impact on Information Systems Misuse: A Deterrence Approach", *Information Systems Research*, 17(1), 2009, 79–98.

Dhillon, G., and J. Backhouse, "Current Directions in IS Security Research: Towards Socio-organizational

Perspectives", *Information Systems Journal*, 11(2), 2001, 127–153.

Duhigg, C., *The Power of Habit: Why We Do What We Do and How to Change*, Random House, 2013.

Etzioni, Amitai, *Moral Dimension: Toward a New Economics*, Simon and Schuster, 2010.

Fléchais, I. "Designing Secure and Usable Systems", PhD dissertation, University College London, 2005.

Flechais, I., J. Riegelsberger and M. A. Sasse, "Divide and Conquer: The Role of Trust and Assurance in the Design of Secure Socio-technical Systems", in Proceedings of the 2005 Workshop on New Security Paradigms (NSPW '05). ACM, New York, NY, USA, 33–41, 2005.

Flechais, I., M. A. Sasse and S. M. V. Hailes. "Bringing Security Home: A Process for Developing Secure and Usable Systems", in *ACM/SIGSAC New Security Paradigms Workshop*, ACM, New York, NY, USA, 49.-57, 2003.

Freeman, R. E., and McVea J., "A Stakeholder Approach to Strategic Management", Darden Business School Working Paper No. 01-02, 2001.

Friedman, B., D. C. Howe and E. Felten, "Informed Consent in the Mozilla Browser: Implementing Value-Sensitive Design", in System Sciences, 2002. HICSS. Proceedings of the 35th Annual Hawaii International Conference on System Sciences. IEEE (2002).

Sources

Fulford, H, and N. F. Doherty, "The Application of Information Security Policies in Large UK-Based Organizations: An Exploratory Investigation", *Information Management & Computer Security*, 11(3), 2003, 106–114.

Furnell, S. M., A. Jusoh and D. Katsabas, "The Challenges of Understanding and Using Security: A Survey of End-Users", *Computers & Security*, 25(1), 2006, 27–35.

Garfinkel, S. L., and A. Shelat, "Remembrance of Data Passed: A Study of Disk Sanitization Practices", *IEEE Security & Privacy*, 1, 2003, 17–27.

Gino, F., Ayal, S., and Ariely, D., "Contagion and Differentiation in Unethical Behavior: The Effect of One Bad Apple on the Barrel", *Psychological Science*, 20(3), 2009, 393–398.

Gladwell, M., *The Tipping Point: How Little Things Can Make a Big Difference*, Little, Brown, 2006.

Gordon, L. A. and Martin P. L., *Managing Cybersecurity Resources: A Cost–Benefit Analysis*, Mcgraw-Hill.

Greenwald, S. J., Olthoff K.G., Raskin V., and Ruch, W., "The User Non-acceptance Paradigm: INFOSEC's Dirty Little Secret", *Proceedings of the New Security Paradigms Workshop*, 2004.

Hamel, G., and Prahalad C. K., *Competing for the Future*, Harvard Business Press, 2013.

Hemantha, S. B. Herath and Tehaswini C. Herath, "Cyber-Insurance: Copula Pricing Framework and Implications for Risk Management", *Proceedings of*

Sources

the Sixth Workshop on the Economics of Information Security, Carnegie Mellon University, 7–8 June 2007.

Herley, C., "So Long, and No Thanks for the Externalities: The Rational Rejection of Security Advice by Users", in Proceedings of the 2009 workshop on New security paradigms workshop (NSPW '09). ACM, New York, NY, USA, 133–144 (2009).

Herzberg, F., Mausner, B., and Snyderman, B. B., *The Motivation to Work*, new edn, Transaction, 1993.

Higgins, H. N., "Corporate System Security: Towards an Integrated Management Approach", *Information Management and computer Security*, 7(5), 1999, 217–222.

Huang, D., Q. Hu and R. Behara, "Economics of Information Security Investment in the Case of Simultaneous Attacks, *Proceedings of the Fifth Workshop on the Economics of Information Security*, Cambridge University, 26–28 June 2006.

Inglesant, P. G., and M. A. Sasse, "The True Cost of Unusable Password Policies: Password Use in the Wild", in Proceedings of the 28th International Conference on Human Factors in Computing Systems, 2010, Atlanta, GA: ACM, 383–392.

James., H. L., "Managing Information Systems Security: A Soft Approach", in Proceedings of the 1996 Information Systems Conference of New Zealand (ISCNZ '96). IEEE Computer Society, Washington, DC, 1996.

Sources

Johnson, E., and E. Goetz, "Embedding Information Security into the Organisation", *IEEE Security & Privacy*, 3, May–June 2007, 16–24.

Johnson, E., and S. Dynes, "Inadvertent Disclosure: Information Leaks in Extended Enterprise", Proceedings of the Sixth Workshop on the Economics of Information Security, Carnegie Mellon University, 7–8 June 2007.

Kahneman, D., and Tversky, A., "Prospect Theory: An Analysis of Decision under Risk", *Econometrica*, 47(2), March 1979, 263–291.

Karyda, M., E. Kiountouzis and S. Kokolakis, "Information Systems Security Policies: A Contextual Perspective", *Computers & Security* 24(3), 2005, 246–260.

Kirlappos, I, Beautement, A., and Sasse, A. M., "'Comply or Die' Is Dead: Long Live Security-Aware Principal Agents", in *Financial Cryptography and Data Security*, Springer, 2013, 70–82.

Kirlappos, I., and M. A. Sasse, "Security Education against Phishing: A Modest Proposal for a Major Rethink", *Security & Privacy, IEEE*, 10(2), 2012, 24–32.

Klein, Gary, *Streetlights and Shadows: Searching for the Keys to Adaptive Decision Making*, MIT Press, 2009.

Kumar, V., R. Telang and T. Mukhopahhyay, "Optimally Securing Interconnected Information Systems and Assets", Proceedings of the Sixth Workshop on *the*

Sources

Economics of Information Security, Carnegie Mellon University, 7–8 June 2007.

Maeda, J, *The Laws of Simplicity*, MIT Press, 2006.

Mehrabian, A., and Ferris, S. R., "Inference of Attitudes from Nonverbal Communication in Two Channels", *Journal of Consulting Psychology*, 31(3), 1967, 248–252.

Mitchell, R. K., Agle, B. R., and Wood, D. J., "Toward a Theory of Stakeholder Identification and Salience: Defining the Principle of Who and What Really Counts", *Academy of Management Review*, 22(4), 1997, 853–886.

Nielsen, J., "Iterative User Interface Design", *IEEE Computer*, 26(11) (1993), 32–41.

Norman, D. A., "Some Observations on Mental Models", in D. A. Gentner and A. A. Stevens, eds., *Mental Models*, Erlbaum, 1993.

Ohno, T., *Toyota Production System: Beyond Large-Scale Production*, Productivity Press, 1988.

Plattner, H., Meinel, C., and Leifer, L. J., eds., *Design Thinking: Understand–Improve–Apply.* Springer Science & Business Media, 2010.

Popper, K. R., "Of Clocks and Clouds: An Approach to the Problem of Rationality and the Freedom of Man," in *Objective Knowledge: An Evolutionary Approach*, Clarendon Press, 1972, 206–265.

Reis, E., *The Lean Startup*, Crown Business, 2011.

Sources

Rittel, Horst W. J., and Webber, M. M., "Dilemmas in a General Theory of Planning", *Policy Sciences*, 4, 1973, 155–169.

Sasse, M. A., S. Brostoff and Weirich, D., "Transforming the 'Weakest Link': A Human–Computer Interaction Approach to Usable and Effective Security", *BT Technology Journal*, 19(3), July 2001, 122–131.

Schlienger, T., and Teufel, S., "Analyzing Information Security Culture: Increased Trust by an Appropriate Information Security Culture", in Proceedings of the 14th International Workshop on Database and Expert Systems Applications, IEEE, 2003, 405–409.

Schneier, B., *Secrets and Lies: Digital Security in a Networked World*, Wiley, 2000.

Schneier, B., *Beyond Fear: Thinking Sensibly about Security in an Uncertain World*, Copernicus Books, 2003.

Schuler, D., and Namioka, A., *Participatory Design: Principles and Practices*, CRC Press, 1993.

Scott M. M., "Who Are Your Motivated Workers?", *Harvard Business Review*, 1964, 73-88

Sharma, D. N., and P. K. Dash, "Effectiveness of ISO 27001, as an Information Security Management System: An Analytical Study of Financial Aspects", *Far East Journal of Psychology and Business*, 9(5), 2012, 57–71.

Sherwood, J., Clark, A., and Lynas, D., "Enterprise Security Architecture White Paper", 2009.

Sources

Shiv, B., and Fedorikhin, A., "Heart and Mind in Conflict: The Interplay of Affect and Cognition in Consumer Decision Making", *Journal of Consumer Research*, 1999, 278–292.

Son, J-Y., "Out of Fear or Desire? Toward a Better Understanding of Employees' Motivation to Follow IS Security Policies", *Information Management*, 48(7), 2011, 296–302.

Strauss, A., and Corbin, J., *Basics of Qualitative Research: Techniques and Procedures for Developing Grounded Theory*, Sage Publications Incorporated, 2007.

Taleb, N. N., *The Black Swan: The Impact of the Highly Improbable Fragility*, Vol. 2, Random House, 2010.

Trompeter, C. M., and Eloff, J. H. P., "A Framework for the Implementation of Socio-ethical Controls in Information Security", *Computers & Security*, 20(5), 2001, 384–391.

Von Solms, B., and Von Solms, R., "From Information Security to Business Security", *Computers & Security*, 24(4), 271–273 (2005).

Vroom, C., and Von Solms, R., "Towards Information Security Behavioural Compliance", *Computers & Security*, 23(3), 2004, 191–198.

Wash, R., "Folk Models of Home Computer Security", Proceedings of the Sixth Symposium on Usable Privacy and Security, ACM, 2010.

Weirich, D., and Sasse, M. A., "Pretty Good Persuasion: A First Step towards Effective Password Security for the Real World", Proceedings of the New Security Paradigms Workshop, 10–13 September 2001, Cloudcroft, NM: ACM Press, 137–143.

Whitten, A., and Tygar, J. D., "Why Johnny Can't Encrypt: A Usability Evaluation of PGP 5.0", Proceedings of the 8th USENIX Security Symposium, August 1999, Washington, DC, 1999.

Wilson, J. Q., and Kelling, G. L., "Broken Windows: The Police and Neighborhood Safety", *The Atlantic*, 29(31), 1982, 29–38.

Wilson, T., *Strangers to Ourselves*, Harvard University Press, 2004.

Wood, C. C., "An Unappreciated Reason Why Information Security Policies Fail", *Computer Fraud & Security*, 10, 2000, 13–14.

Yee, K. P., "User Interaction Design for Secure Systems", in L. Faith Cranor and S. Garfinkel, eds., *Security and Usability: Designing Secure Systems That People Can Use 2005*, O'Reilly Books, 13–30.

Zinatullin, L., "Modelling Conflicts between Security Compliance and Human Behaviour", dissertation, University College London, 2013.

Zurko, M. E., and Simon, R. T., "User-Centered Security", New Security Paradigms Workshop 1997

ITG RESOURCES

IT Governance Ltd sources, creates and delivers products and services to meet the real-world, evolving IT governance needs of today's organisations, directors, managers and practitioners.

The ITG website (*www.itgovernance.co.uk*) is the international one-stop-shop for corporate and IT governance information, advice, guidance, books, tools, training and consultancy.

Publishing Services

IT Governance Publishing (ITGP) is the world's leading IT-GRC publishing imprint that is wholly owned by IT Governance Ltd.

With books and tools covering all IT governance, risk and compliance frameworks, we are the publisher of choice for authors and distributors alike, producing unique and practical publications of the highest quality, in the latest formats available, which readers will find invaluable.

www.itgovernancepublishing.co.uk is the website dedicated to ITGP. Other titles published by ITGP that may be of interest include:

- Build a Security Culture

  www.itgovernance.co.uk/shop/p-1687-build-a-security-culture.aspx

- The Security Consultant's Handbook

www.itgovernance.co.uk/shop/p-1726-the-security-consultants-handbook.aspx

- Information Security: A Practical Guide

  www.itgovernance.co.uk/shop/p-1701-information-security-a-practical-guide-bridging-the-gap-between-it-and-management.aspx

We also offer a range of off-the-shelf toolkits that give comprehensive, customisable documents to help users create the specific documentation they need to properly implement a management system or standard. Written by experienced practitioners and based on the latest best practice, ITGP toolkits can save months of work for organisations working towards compliance with a given standard.

To see the full range of toolkits available please see:

www.itgovernance.co.uk/shop/c-129-toolkits.aspx.

Books and tools published by IT Governance Publishing (ITGP) are available from all business booksellers and the following websites:

www.itgovernance.eu   *www.itgovernanceusa.com*

www.itgovernance.in   *www.itgovernancesa.co.za*

www.itgovernance.asia.

Training Services

Staff training is an essential component of the information security triad of people, processes and technology. IT Governance's ISO27001 Learning Pathway provides information security courses from Foundation to Advanced level, with qualifications awarded by IBITGQ.

Many courses are available in Live Online as well as classroom formats, so delegates can learn and achieve essential career progression from the comfort of their own homes and offices. Delegates passing the exams associated with out ISO27001 Learning Pathway will gain qualifications from IBITGQ, including CIS F, CIS IA, CIS LI, CIS LA, CIS RM and CIS 2013 UP.

For more information about IT Governance's ISO27001 Learning Pathway, please see: *www.itgovernance.co.uk/iso27001-information-security-training.aspx*.

Professional Services and Consultancy

Implementing, maintaining and continually improving an information security management system (ISMS) can be confusing. Companies that focus solely on compliance without appropriately tailoring their security policies to their business needs frequently find their efforts actually provide a poor return on investment: employees can come under strain when poorly implemented security controls prevent them from performing their core business tasks, forcing them to find ways of circumventing security measures, and putting the company at risk.

Fortunately, IT Governance's consultants offer a comprehensive range of flexible, practical project support packages to help organisations of any size, sector or location to implement an ISMS appropriate to their needs while achieving certification to ISO 27001.

For more information on our ISO 27001 consultancy service, please see:
www.itgovernance.co.uk/iso27001_consultancy.aspx.

For general information about our other consultancy services, including for ISO20000, ISO22301, Cyber Essentials, the PCI DSS, data protection and more, please see: *www.itgovernance.co.uk/consulting.aspx*.

Newsletter

IT governance is one of the hottest topics in business today, not least because it is also the fastest moving.

You can stay up to date with the latest developments across the whole spectrum of IT governance subject matter, including; risk management, information security, ITIL and IT service management, project governance, compliance and so much more, by subscribing to ITG's core publications and topic alert emails.

Simply visit our subscription centre and select your preferences: *www.itgovernance.co.uk/newsletter.aspx*.